The Law of Nutrition

Master Beinsa Douno

CONTENTS

DIGESTIVE SYSTEM

Each organ has its own purpose. At least – each organ is a reflection of those forces, which act in a certain area, where the organ itself acts. Today's science is on a right path. It studies the types of services, provided by the nerves, blood vessels, veins and arteries, what part the heart plays in the blood circulation etc. But science cannot make an analogy between the services, rendered by the heart, blood vessels, and other organs in the spiritual world.

Through the brain, lungs, heart, stomach, man connects to angels, cherubs, seraphim.

If, for example, the lungs are not working well, connect with the cherubs – while breathing, think of these spirits and their wisdom.

Through his heart man connects to another hierarchy — the thrones — the heartbeat shows that you are connected to the thrones.

Through his stomach man is connected to the creatures of nobility, therefore, after man has his meal, he becomes more benevolent.

Through his liver man is connected to the powers or the Divine Forces. If there is a disharmony in feelings, yellowing of the face and eyes, then there is a disharmony between the powers and man. Jaundice is treated through restoration of the harmony with the powers.

Through the gall-bladder man is connected to the creatures of goodness. The loss of goodness and the bursting of the gall-bladder are synonyms. In order to reduce all, goodness has to increase.

Through the spleen man is connected to another hierarchy — superiors or Divine Justice. The increase or disruption of the spleen shows that justice is disturbed.

The kidneys are connected to the archangels — the creators of God's Glory – they lead the peoples. Whoever fails to glorify God and be inspired by nature, by greatness in nature, cannot be in connection with the archangels and the kidneys are upset.

Whoever has a healthy and normal digestive system, he is joyful, cheerful, diligent. Should you meet a man with a withered face, yellow, indisposed for work, you can be sure that his digestive system is not working properly. He cannot work, looks at everything gloomily, pessimistically, has not faith in life. In order to avoid such a condition, you should keep your digestive system in good order – this is a precondition for the wellbeing of man in the physical world — the first step of life.

If you consider the stomach and stomach system in a broader sense, you will see that these form a complex machine, which is connected to the complete life.

The celiac plexus or the solar plexus, or the "stomach brain" deals with all the functions of human body. The lower behaviours of man, his perception of good and evil, of joy and fun, all these are due to the stomach brain. The liver is connected with it, and this is one of the greatest servants – one of the assistants of that brain. Sometimes, when this assistant is sick, the entire stomach system is in an improper condition. The digestive system acts incorrectly, and – as a result – inorganic substances accumulate. Blood deposits form in this way as well.

What is the purpose of nutrition? It must first – maintain the body in good order, second – maintain its activity or ability to work, and third – to protect it from the conditions of the environment.

The physical world is the abdomen of man, which consists of three areas: hell —the large intestine, purgatory— the small intestines and heaven – the stomach.

Hell is situated in the intestines of man. That is why, when a doctor has to treat somebody, he first cleans his intestine.

The stomach provides the necessary materials for the construction of the human body, i.e. of the physical man. It participates actively in the construction of the body.

The building material, which is then allocated in the entire body, is stored in the stomach.

The stomach is the centre of the physical power of man. The strong one has an excellent stomach — it depends on the proper functioning of the sympathetic nervous system.

If you act properly in the material works, your digestive system will work properly.

You are responsible to your stomach, for the food, you take through your mouth.

How will you eat, if your stomach is upset? You have everything to eat, but your stomach would not accept anything. Everyone with a disordered stomach, should know that Justice is not in his heart, Truth is not in his mind. In order to fix his stomach, one has to bring Justice into his heart and Truth to your mind. This must happen by all means, so that the stomach can digest food and process the juices, required for supporting the body. The truth is that in its simplest form, necessary for restoring the balance of the body, it keeps the digestive system in good order.

Justice keeps the heart and lungs in good order. If there is no Justice, the heart and lungs will suffer.

The reason for all the ulcers in the stomach is the lie. Lie alters the chemical composition of the blood and tissues in the body.

If the stomach system of a person is well developed, he cannot resist great temptations and behaves amorally — he eats a lot, drinks a lot. He is not capable of transforming his physical energies into spiritual ones.

The good deeds maintain the healthy condition of the stomach system, and as a result one eats and sleeps well.

Act justly, so that your stomach works properly

Whoever has a healthy stomach, he is a good man.

Stomach defines the desires of a man.

A person's love of people regulates his stomach. If you have a healthy stomach, your love of people is correct. If your stomach aches, your love of people is not proper.

When a man loves, his stomach expands, when he hates – his stomach shrinks.

A man with a sick stomach, cannot love. Him, who has a sick chest or a sick brain cannot love either.

Animals support the stomach system. Whoever wants to have a healthy and well regulated stomach system, must be reasonable and create proper relations with the animals.

The more cheek-bones protrude, and cheeks sink-in, the weaker one's stomach system is. When the stomach system is weak, one succumbs to pessimistic conditions This is due to the fact that digestion does not take place properly. In order not to be overwhelmed with pessimism, through the power of your will, you must work to improve your stomach system.

If your stomach suffers, if a number of generations had suffered from their stomach system, hollow lines form on the face. When the stomach starts suffering indentions form on the face. When the stomach is healthy, these lines straighten and people become a bit stouter.

If the lower part of the nose is thick, this shows that the stomach is well developed. The duration of man's life depends on that.

The length of the arm from the shoulder to the elbow represents the material world, or the stomach, from the elbow to the wrist – this is the spiritual world, the heart, and the wrist – the mental world, the mind.

The upper arm corresponds to the stomach, to the belly. If this part of the arm is thick, then the stomach is well developed.

The people, whose stomach is developed, have well developed finger bases. When the belly prevails, the finger bases prevail as well. When stomach is weak, fingers are weak as well.

All people, in whim the belly is developed, have thick finger bases, without interspaces. Such people love to indulge themselves. And all those, with underdeveloped stomach system, have their first phalanx of the forefinger, here, below, a bit dry.

When eyes start sinking, stomach starts getting worse. The one, who has good eyes, has a healthy stomach. The stomach is connected to vision. The stomach is connected with the longs, it is connected with the brain. One's eyes can show if that person is smart, one's eyes can also show if that person's healthy in his lungs, eyes can show if the stomach system is normal.

Some have glassy, sharp eyes which are not moist, people say: "He has glassy eyes". His nervous system is upset. His eyes are misty the stomach system is upset. You have no experience. When your stomach aches, you will see that your eyes become misty.

When one's eyes seem lighter, this shows the condition of his mind, and when they look darker – this shows the condition of his stomach.

Often our eyes become bad, due to the food we eat. If the food is unhealthy, it corrupts the blood, and corrupted blood damages the eyes and then surgeries are necessary. Why? Our lives conform to God's laws. As lamination occurs in the physical eye, similar lamination occurs in the spiritual eye, according to that law, and this lamination causes misery for both the individual, and the family, society, the nation and the entire mankind.

If a vegetarian has misty eyes, the reason for that is the excess amount of sugar in his body. Nervous people worry for no real reason, for the air that they breathe. Sometimes an offensive word, said by someone, disturbs you so much that for 20 years you cannot forget that. And if someone says that you are a simpleton, you get angry and can't get that word out of your mind for days, months and years.

Americans are very active. They apply everything, but there are many systems, which have no application. In terms of hygiene, their very inconsistent. If you go to a winter party or dance in America, you will find yourselves at your wits' end. You will be offered a 150 g. cup of ice-cream and then they will serve you a 250 g. cup of hot coffee. And when you look at these Americans, all their teeth are golden – they have not a single healthy tooth in their mouths. With these sudden changes between cold and hot, the enamel cracks. Many of them suffer from dyspepsia. Do you know what kind of disease dyspepsia is? This is a severe condition. Whoever suffers from dyspepsia, falls in a very poor condition, in hypochondria, he does not want to live, he can't sleep, bad dreams bother him constantly, everything turns upside-down. I refer to this condition as a disorder of the sympathetic nervous system. This is not the result of an evil will.

Some American psychologists explain to some extend these bad conditions with the indiscriminate extermination of the Indians, when Europeans came to America. And these spirits of those killed, now seek revenge. These are not scientific facts, but just allegations, these are only opinions. In one relation Americans are very pure, they maintain extreme hygiene in their lives, but on the other hand, they are great meat-eaters.

Stomach is supported by many organs: the teeth, tongue, mouth, gullet, intestines.

The white color of the teeth speaks of virtues. Whoever has white, nice teeth, he is a man of virtues.

Those of you, who believe that you will come again in the future, should pray to God to give you healthy teeth. If it is impossible now, you will have them in the future. If you go to the other world, you'd want to have strong teeth there. If you don't have healthy teeth there, you will be banished. They don't accept people without teeth in the other world.

Sometimes man likes to bite – this is another issue, a habit acquired from the animal kingdom, from those animals, who didn't understand their purpose. A man who bites, does not know how to play. I have looked at many, who, when sawing, don't use scissors, but bite the thread to cut it, they use their teeth to break walnuts. They break one tooth, damage another. Don't break nuts with your teeth! Then, in order for the teeth to be healthy and strong, you must not eat your soup while hot. You'd want, when you come to the Earth, not to eat any soup. It damages your teeth. You drink hot water, drink cold water, then the enamel cracks, and teeth are damaged.

When you know how to eat well, your teeth will be strong and healthy and you'll be a king. When your teeth fall, you've been fire, you become a pensioner.

Never eat or drink anything cold after having something hot and vice-versa, for this is how teeth are most easily damaged. If teeth are damaged, the stomach is also damaged and then the brain system. The destruction of teeth is related to the cerebellum. When the cerebellum is not functioning properly, when the liver is not functioning properly, the teeth start deteriorating and thus make things worse. Everything can get worse, due to ignorance, incomprehension. With our worries, with our disbelief, with the violence that we reveal, we only make our lives more complicated.

Nowadays few people enjoy good teeth. The reason for the early deterioration or falling off of the teeth is the life of former generations. They lived in a way damaging their gums.

When electricity connects properly with magnetism, it produces regular shapes, the tone is right. If not all of them join in one, then there is a discord, the tone is not true. If there are 32 oscillations, 16 are positive and 16 are negative.

Now some may say: "Why should we bother about music?" Well, you eat, and that is music. You have 32 teeth, each tooth has an individual tone. The teeth form a harp. Sometimes people lose their teeth, then a discord is produced. The improper life damages people's bones and teeth.

Teeth should not always be brushed – it is enough to wash them with warm water and soap or some alcohol. Many diseases are caused by the germs, which develop in teeth.

When you chew mastic, you unconsciously clean your teeth, and at the same time you fill your gums with blood and thus the teeth are fed and strengthened.

When teeth go bad, the heart goes bad as well.

You should alternate the left and right side, while you eat, and you should eat slowly and chew well, so that you get good results. If you only chew on the left side, you will become very sensitive, and if you only chew on your right side, you will only develop your thought. In order to achieve harmony between your thoughts and feelings and achieve inner peace, you should chew now on your right side and now on you left.

He, who can't think, he has bad teeth.

People say about someone: "His lips are beautiful as a rose". What are the lips? They express human heart — they show if one is warm- or cold-hearted, how communicative and frank he is. You will notice that those who have good appetite have rather thick lips. This is a physiological law.

More blood flows in the lips and that is why they are both thick and red.

The lips reflect the digestive system. If the lower lip is thicker, if the perceptions are stronger, this shows that the person with the thicker lower lip is rather a passive person, a person of perceptions. If the upper lip is thicker, that the person is more active. If perceptions are stronger, than he would consume more food.

When you get up in the morning, you should take a look at your face, reflect a little on your appearance, and when you notice a defect in you, you should correct it immediately. If your lip has become a little twisted, or if your mouth is black – the lack of beauty is a measure, you should always look at the color of your mouth. Stick out our tongue – if it is whitish, this is not a good sign. Your tongue should be red. Stick it out, look in the mirror to check if it is red or white. If the tongue gets white, you are getting older. When the tongue is getting red, then you are getting younger. The white tongue shows that the digestion is not right. Then you should try to improve your stomach so that your tongue gets better as well.

The tongue is connected to the sense of smell. It has three functions: first – it tastes food, this is the inspector, who checks things. Tongue's second function is to turn the food around. Its third function is to speak. Thoughts are expressed through speech.

The cells of the tongue perceive the oscillations of food and give us an idea of the various types of food.

One's tongue has to be so sensitive that it can distinguish the quality of water. For this purpose one has to experiment, to go to the mountains and drink water from clean springs, then he has to compare different types of water so that he can develop an expert sense in order to identify the water quality.

The small blisters, appearing on your tongue, are the result of some bad words that you have said about your friends.

In the human development, one of the first senses that have appeared is the sense of appetite, zest, desire to eat. This centre is situated in front of the ears. Thanks to that centre, man has the desire to try, to taste things, that is why the mouth has appeared.

Mouth is the original manifestation of the human being.

Mouth is stomach's door.

Mouth is the expression of feelings. The taste and health of a person also depend on the mouth. If you have a mouth, you feel well, you speak well and eat well.

Mouth solves a lot of issues. It is enough to eat properly and speak reasonably in order to deal successfully with a lot of difficulties.

What is important is the distance between the eyes and the mouth. Personality changes as the distance between the mouth and the eyes gets shorter. If the mouth is further from the eyes, one's personality takes another direction. If the mouth is in the focus, everything you see is perceived simultaneously with all the other organs – through your tongue, nose, ear. This is how you understand that you see and know things.

When the temple areas of someone are well developed, similarly developed are also the lips. There is a correlation between the human temples and lips. The better developed the temple areas are, the thicker the lips become. This can be notices especially in people, who have their nose near the lips. Because the nose is related to the sense of smell, every time a nice dish is smelled, the nose promotes a blood flow to the lips, thus making them thicker.

Mouth is the centre of certain energy. Mouth is separated in two parts of a specific radius. It is strictly established how big the human mouth can be. It depends also on the size of the stomach — on the ability to eat more or less. The thickness of the lips shows one's predisposition to eating.

When your lips become very thin, you will stop sensing the taste of fruits, of food The people, who have good appetite, have thick lips and the reason for that is this: because they feel the food, more blood flows to the lips.

When the lips are thick, well developed, this means that this person has a well developed appetite and sensuality. When the lips are thin, the sensuality is not developed well.

The bigger one's mouth, the closer his desires are, the smaller the mouth – the further his desires, i.e. his objects are far.

Your appetite can be determined, based on the opening of your mouth. The wider the mouth opens, the hungrier you are.

The mouth of which of you does not smell, tell me that! You must clean your mouth and teeth constantly – washing your mouth even ten times a day is not enough.

Your breath smells, because you don't give properly, or because your stomach is not well.

You must wash your mouth constantly, so that you don't make it possible for poisons to form in the channels. The mouth and hands must always be clean.

You throw away your saliva in such an outrageous way, and sometimes it can be healing.

If your knee aches, start spitting on it – 4-5-100 times – you'll see that there will be a change. Try it – this medicine is free. Didn't Christ heal the blind with spittle and mud!

You have a wound. Put some spittle on your wound, cover it with cotton or gauze and it will heal. Don't pick at it.

You get bitten by a mosquito — spit on the bitten place. Also, if someone insults you, put some spittle on the ear, with which you heard the insult. If you can't solve a problem, spit on your finger and put it on your forehead. If you can't remember something, spit on your finger and put it in the middle of your forehead, where the centre of memory is located.

The composition of saliva changes every minute and it defines the changes, happening in one's mind. This is a field of science, which will be studied in the future.

In order to know how permanent or transient your achievements are, you should study your mouth. How long will you live – this can be told by your mouth, your tongue, and, in particular, by the taste. If everything you taste, is accepted without any conflict and with a good disposition, you will continue your life.

Until several years ago, scholars were unable to determine the function of the blind gut and that is why they maintained that the blind gut, as a remnant of the past, may be cut and thrown away. In the US there was a habit of cutting away children's blind guts, but they noticed that this resulted in constipation, digestion didn't happen properly. They used to poison children in this way. The modern physiologists have determined that the blind gut helped the small and large intestines to separate the impurities more easily. However if someone's blind gut is cut away, that man was destined to new suffering.

The blind gut helps the small and large intestines to separate the impurities more easily, if it is cut away, then constipation and a lot of other sufferings start. There is no organ in human body, which is useless — all of them have their great purposes. A lot of the past and current sufferings of people are due to the fact that they failed to everything necessary to fully use the organs that God gave them.

From the navel down man is regulated by the centre of the Earth, and from the navel up – from the centre of the sun. If we are not in harmony with the earth, than our digestion is pure. When we are in harmony with the earth, then our digestion works fine. One has to be in harmony with the Earth. I consider the Earth a reasonable factor.

There are two diameters in a circle, and they are equal. However the ellipse has two diameters, which are not equal. One is longer, the other is shorter. What does that mean? The shape of men is not round, but elliptic. Therefore a men's length, aligned with the earth is perpendicular. Man is perpendicular to the centre of the Sun and the centre of the Earth. This shows his intelligence. The length of this ellipse shows his reasonableness, and the width shows his sensitivity.

Animals have the reverse process — their feelings are wider, than their intelligence. Animals differ from the people by having more feelings than they need. Man has more reason and less feeling than he needs. And then there should be some relations, an exchange between animals and people. When people don't know how to make this business exchange, they start to slaughter animals and eat them. They eat animals to take their feelings, i.e. to get what they lack. But they have started along the wrong path, this is a misunderstanding. On the other hand, animals, when they need more intelligence, they also eat people, to get what they lack. Animals eat people and people eat animals. However neither the animals have become smarter, nor have people become more sensitive.

LIVER AND GALL BLADDER

What is liver? Liver is that matter, which has created the world. The Lord has created the world through the liver. What would you say to that? Do you know what acids, what powers acted during the creation of the liver? It will release them. Then it will say to the others: "I did my job ".

When someone is told that God first created the world through the liver, and then he created man, this will seem inexplicable and impossible. Because liver was able to create, the Lord assigned him once again with that job. The Lord told him: "There's no other organ like you, which can do that job – to serve digestion and support life ". What are the scientific arguments, which can prove this great significance of liver? I can prove that to you. When you look at someone, who has a disordered liver, what do you see? That man is all yellow. If you marry a woman with a disturbed liver, you will have to suffer. The best people in the world are those with healthy livers.

A person lives in four bodies: physical, astral, mental and causal. Each body performs certain work and is formed of a specific matter, and each organ of the physical body is connected to the respective astral organ, i.e. to the world of feelings. The liver regulates the lower feelings of men, ingests the poisons of the human body and transforms them. If it is disordered, the poisons spread throughout the body and one dies.

The spiritual heart is located in the pit of the stomach and it is called "solar plexus" — it is the most tender area, which one has to protect. The solar plexus is under the influence of the liver. All the filth of the mental and cardiac world goes to the liver, and from there – to the centre of the Earth, where it is purified. Therefore, the solar plexus serves as a channel for the purification of unclean thoughts and desires. One's heart depends on the condition of his liver.

The lungs and liver are two transformers of energies – the lungs transform mental energy, they direct the mental energy towards the brain, and the liver transforms the sensual energies, directing them to the sympathetic nervous system. Feelings cannot be expressed without the liver.

The energies of the heart pass through the liver, there is an open path there, however there is no path from the liver to the heart. That is why you should never allow any negative feelings and energies in your hearts, which may affect negatively your liver.

When the solar, mental and sympathetic systems do not function properly, black circles are formed around one's eyes – this happens also when the liver is overexcited. Liver is an undertaking in nature, where all the lower feelings are formed. The animal conditions, which are observed in animals, are all due to the liver. Our indisposition is due to the liver. It must function properly. It has two functions, two jobs to do: it helps digestion, and at the same time these animal feelings are all due to it. It is close, next to the stomach brain or the solar plexus.

When does the liver stop working well? It fails due to intensive feeling that you have. For example – when one accommodates utter self-esteem and fear at the same time – these are two countering forces. The utterly offended person wants revenge, and at the same time there's fear. He wants revenge, but can't achieve it. Fear holds him. Than that fear affects one's liver. Every day personal feelings arise in people, every day fear arises.

If one's liver is disordered, negative, unpleasant thoughts pass through one's mind. The disorder of the liver results in cruelty. The liver is related to the lower feelings. Knowing that, one must protect his holy God-given health.

In the spiritual world, the liver presents all those materials, from which feelings are made.

Feelings also affect the liver's health.

Liver is necessary, but if it increases excessively, disasters may occur. To be too small is bad either. Liver must function properly and produce bile.

If one's liver is disordered, that man is bankrupt. With the current structure of the body, everything depends on the liver.

Liver is a great factor in human body. If the liver is damaged, that man is broke. (...) If liver is disordered, one becomes indisposed, gloomy, pessimistic, unable to talk kindly, he starts hating, fighting, and might even commit a murder — all this is caused by the liver. And if there are so many criminals in the modern world, the main reason for that is people's livers are disordered. Fix their livers!

The insult, you live with, affects your liver, as a bitter feeling, which cannot be easily overcome. The good and bad condition of the liver affects feelings, and feelings affect the health of the liver. If it does not work well, one is nervous, easily gets angry or irritated. If someone says that he does not want to eat, that he can't stand anybody around him, that he cannot get along with anybody, trusts nobody and does not believe in God, this is all liver's fault. The liver is a small organ, which plays a very important role. It has an enormous effect on one's mentality.

As long as liver is connected to creatures of the lower astral world, they start influencing a person, whispering to him pessimistic philosophy or making him commit suicide. These creatures are strong, but they are not well organized. Not understanding life, they are ready to kill anybody, who is in their way. If you find yourselves in a miserable spiritual state, you will know that you are in the area of the unorganized matter. All the saints have healthy livers, well organized lower feelings. The organized liver is the best servant of the heart.

Whenever the liver is functioning properly, the complexion of the face is pleasant and pink.

If you see one's face starting to turn yellow or red, you should try to find the reason in the liver first.

The disorder of the liver causes various diseases. Neurasthenia is also caused by a disorder of the liver. Whoever is not ready to help people, who are not in communion with God, he is sick, his liver is disordered. When you're angry turn to God and ask him to give you more knowledge and light, so that you can set your liver straight. If you can't stand people, if your life is not going well, if you're not able to learn, this is again your liver's fault. Its disorder affects the mental abilities and feelings of men, as well as his spiritual manifestations. The lower feelings affect liver, like termites devouring everything.

Whoever has managed to organize his feelings and thoughts, he has also organized his liver. His can make peace with everybody. You see how important liver is for everybody, it is also related to faith. If you believe in God, then you have an organized liver, this means that you have an organized mind, heart and soul. By "faith in God" I mean a divine condition, where one feels strong enough to achieve everything he wants. Faith is a force which can achieve everything — it is necessary for the organization of the liver.

If the liver becomes sick, it is hard to heal; it is connected to the cerebellum.

All the doctors admit one thing: it is very hard to heal the liver. They know that if one contracts jaundice, it is difficult to cure him and the reason for that is liver. When the stomach is disordered, once again the reason is the liver. If the nervous system is disordered – again liver is the reason. If you are irritable or angry, the liver is the reason. You scold, reason is in the liver. When you set the liver right, you become a saint right away. Some saints, wise men, spent 20 years in the dessert, in order to deal with their liver.

Many of the diseases are the result of liver disorders. When it does not function properly, this results in damages to the body, diseases occur, which are hard to cure: hypochondria is the result of a liver disorder, neurasthenia is the result of a liver disorder, bad digestion is the result of a liver disorder.

You should keep the liver in a straight-up position, that you will not be nervous, intemperate. There are many specialties for treating liver, but I tell you to think and puts some lemon in your mouth, I give you the most harmless medicines.

When liver gets sick, you will talk to it, as if it is a rational being; you will talk to it every night, asking it to get well.

Scholars don't know that if someone does not like any of his organs, that organ will be disordered. The liver is disordered. Why is that? Because you don't like it. It gets angry and starts destroying itself. Start loving the liver and it will get better. The best heal-of for the liver is to love it and, knowing its importance, it will get better. If you start loving also the inconsistencies, you will keep your liver in perfect order. If you think the world is not functioning properly, you distress your liver. In this way you harm yourselves. Liver contains everything food, but what harms man is that does not think good of his liver. If you think good of your livers, you will be of benefit to yourselves and to the others.

The cure for the sick liver is: don't hate anybody! There is a lurking hatred, which disorders the liver.

So here's what I say: if digestion is not taking place properly and the eyes get yellow, then the liver is not fine. There was time when liver used to think. All the hatred and malice in men originates in liver. When someone hates you, he cannot hate you with his mind, but from the liver, which is thus disordered. Each case of hatred, of ill feelings, is connected to one's liver. And being filled with hatred, the liver cannot perform its functions, digestions does not take place properly.

You may ask: "How should we cure our livers?" You must breathe deeply and eat lemons, and not get angry. You all have a body, showing you precisely what you need.

When somebody loses his purity, his eyes get yellow, the liver is disordered. Then you should start healing it, massaging it.

"I don't want to live anymore!" This is a strange philosophy. The reason is that there's an inert matter in you. Where is it? It is either in your liver, or in your stomach or in your blood circulation or in your heart, or in your respiratory system or in the brain. This is where it is. You should search for the reason. Then, if your liver is disturbed, you need more citric acid. This citric acid can be obtained from light. You should know which ray of the sun you must use: red, orange, green, yellow, light blue, dark blue or violet and to know how to collect that light in order to send it to the liver.

The yellow color, which is in the mental world, if transferred to the physical world, means shows a certain physical disorder. If transferred to the body, it disorders the liver. The yellow color strengthens the brain, but disorders the liver. Therefore many people suffer from liver disorders, because they do not think. When one starts thinking, it is the thought that can consume the yellow color from the mind and put to work.

If the liver is disordered, you should only drink warm water and lemons. A person may want to set everything about him in order, to get his life going , and then start living, but while doing that he disorders his liver.

20

There is a close connection between the liver the gall-bladder. If this connection is interrupted, life is in danger.

When bile is excreted on time and where necessary, it helps digestion. If, however, the gall-bladder does not function properly, this makes a person suffer from dangerous diseases.

When one is angry, irritated, excited, the gall-bladder does not function properly, resulting in various disorders of the body.

In order to transform his feelings and assimilate as he should the bile, man must eat such food that seems good to him, mainly fruits.

The human gall-bladder is under the influence of Mars. According to some astrologists the motion of the gall bladder coincides with the motion of Mars.

RELATIONS

Eating is related to the sympathetic nervous system, to the human feelings. Eating in general is not part of the physical world, but of a higher world. The simple movements are part of the physical world. Eating, however, is belongs to a higher culture. In order to know how to eat, one has to be of a higher culture.

Where eating is not proper, no success, no culture can exist. Eating is the basis of the physical field. The main reason for all misfortunes that now exist or will exist in the future, are due to eating. Of course, eating is related to a number of other processes. If eating is not right, the process of breathing, which is a very important process, will also be incorrect. If breathing, as an important process, is not right, thought also develops incorrectly. Eating is also related to the process of Love. You often talk about Love, but you must know that whoever can't eat right, he can't love either. Everybody who doesn't eat properly, has their sympathetic nervous disordered, and – as a result – they are nervous, choleric, angry. Therefore, neurasthenia is nothing but a result of improper eating. Whoever wants to cure his nervousness, must first learn how to eat properly and use proper food.

We say: "Man must live". In order for man to be able to live on the Earth, he must have an excellent stomach, excellent chest, lungs and an excellently working brain. These are three doors, through which the Divine benediction can enter. A benediction will enter the stomach through the mouth. Another benediction will enter the chest through the lungs, and through the nervous system, through the eyes the Divine benedictions will enter from the outside.

Three factors take part in one's nutrition. The first factor is the stomach. It supplies the materials – food for the entire body. The second factor is the lungs, which receive air from the mouth and uses it to purify, i.e. oxidize blood. The third factor is the brain, which sends energy to the entire body.

First, you must ask yourselves the question, what is your attitude towards food, towards stomach, what is your attitude towards light, towards your brain. Your happiness, your health depends on that. And not only yours, but also that of your children and wives, of your homes and the thousands future generations. Ann all that has to be learned. What is reasonable in the world, is hidden in the light, the noble feelings one has are hidden in the air, and the good deeds of men are hidden in the good food. Whoever does not know how to eat, can't work well, can't behave well. One who does not know how to behave, can't have noble feelings, and who does not know how to deal with light, he can't think.

The healthy condition of man depends on the interdependence between the head, lungs and stomach.

Thought creates the head of a man, feelings – the heart and lungs, and his deeds – the stomach and bones. Therefore, if one's will declines, the stomach, bones and muscles will also become week. If his feelings decline, the heart and lungs will become week. And if his thought declines, his brain will become week.

Digestion affects blood circulation, circulation affects the respiratory system, the respiratory system affects the nervous system, and it affects the brain – the headquarters of thought. If all processes are performed correctly that will make thought correct as well.

A normal person always eats reasonably, without letting himself feel heaviness in his stomach. A normal person always breaths deeply and rhythmically, without choking. A normal person does not know what headache is, never gets disturbed and thinks clearly.

If your brain is not well educated and your feelings are rude, you will spoil what you get from eating and breathing. You may have a wonderful thought and a marvellous feeling, but if you don't eat right, and you don't breathe right, you will nevertheless spoil your health. Than you should out breathing, thinking and feeling into the food. One's health depends on those, as well as the right thinking and progress. When you breathe, you only raise your shoulders and breathe quickly, and this is a tensioning of sorts, and Nature does not like tensioning. You should take your breath slowly, rhythmically, easily. Eating also must incorporate plasticity and music. Some people eat so well, that you feel good watching them do so. When you sit down to eat, imagine that you are sitting for an exam in eating, that you are being observed from the invisible world – they are watching how you sit, how you start eating, how you chew.

Eating makes sense if one is good. If the person is not good, whatever food he uses, he does not have any pleasant sense. He is in the position of the sick person. Whatever he eats, always tastes bitter. In order to be satisfied with his food, one has to be healthy. What's the pleasure of one whose stomach is disordered, while eating. Whatever he puts in his stomach, he will throw it out. One's stomach must be healthy in order to share his desire to eat. This means a proper connection between the head, chest and stomach of a person.

You sit and think wonder what to do. First, you don't know why you are here. You feel that you live, that you are related in a way, that the sun rises and sets, that you are on the Earth. But you don't have a particular idea why are you here. You believe in something, but there's nothing clear in your mind. Your mind holds just a simple idea. You feel that there must be a change in your life, you feel boredom. And you think that the boredom results from the fact that you haven't eaten yet today. So you say: "If I eat, this boredom will go away". And you take bread and put it on the table, and think that you've solved the problem. But once you've eaten that bread, a contrary reaction starts immediately. Instead of becoming active and energetic, you feel ill-disposed and say: "Leave me alone so I can rest!"

Here's what I ask: if this process takes place for the first time, you will find yourself at your wit's end. You'll rest for half an hour on an hour, or even 7 hours at nigh, and feel refreshed, but you'll feel that the problem has not been solved. The emptiness you felt, will still be there.

When you eat, you have this idea in your head: "I am a child, and must grow up ". When you eat, you are now a child. When you breath, then you are an adult. When you start thinking – you are already rational. You eat and don't know why you do it, you breathe and don't know why, you think and you still don't know why. Eating is the outer side of life, breathing is the inner side of life, and thinking is the whole of life. So life has an external and internal side. Only by knowing these two sides, you'll know what the entirety is. The entirety of life is in its perfection.

To it with a good disposition, this means that you are young. In order to enjoy eating, you must be young. There are three persons in the world, who eat with a good disposition: the first one is the young, who has studied and carries love in himself; the second one is the elder person, who has strength; the third is the old one, having acquired sound reason. All the others, who do not fall in either of these categories, can't eat well.

I consider stomach a symbol of the physical world, lungs – a symbol of the spiritual life, and brain –a symbol of the mental life of a person.

The banker is the stomach, the genius – the lungs, and the saint – the head.

I believe one's head cannot ache. The headache is a reflection of what is going on in the stomach. If there is disorder in the stomach — the banker, this is reflected in a headache. There can be no pains in the lungs. They can't be sick. The aches and pains in the lungs are also a reflection of what happens in the stomach. Everything, taking place in the stomach and the intestines bellow the belly-button. This is the lower world, this is hell. You search for hell! The small and large intestines are in hell, all the lower spirits. You will bring order into your hell, you will also bring order into your banker, and not violence. You will teach him that he has to eat moderately, that he must not be very gluttonous. He is a materialist, he says: "I may die hungry if I don't work ". And the banker does not work anything, arms work. Arms and hands belong to the genius, and legs and feet – to the saint, and the banker does nothing. He is given the arms and legs and he has to work with whatever is given to him. The banker says: "I worked for this wheat". The banker thinks that everything that happens in man, is done through him and he says: "Nothing can happen without me ".

Stomach system's job in the physical world is to digest food, and in the spiritual – to deconstruct passions and lower desires of man through digestion. To smash them to small pieces and to send them up to the fireplace. In the physical world heart and lungs purify blood, and in the spiritual world these are the bellows and fireplace, through which all the desires of men must pass in order to separate the clean from the unclean The brain system sends its orders to the various organs for the work they have to do. In the spiritual world the brain sets the job and place of all thoughts in a person. Don't mix pure thoughts with impure. Thought is related to desires, desires to actions, and actions with consequences.

If he eats well, one is healthy, has more resources for work. Whoever eats well, has sound and strong thoughts. The week, sick person can't eat well, and therefore he can't think well. Mind has to be nourished in all three worlds simultaneously: in the divine, spiritual and physical worlds. Eating is not a mechanical process, as many may think. To eat properly means to simultaneously think, feel and perceive the materials, necessary for building something new. The physical person is a servant, the spiritual person – the partner, who has invested his capitals, and the mental person – the one who manages the works.

At first you must think of your head, of your heart and then of your stomach. If you think first of your stomach, then of your heart and head, you are on the wrong path.

If your stomach system does not develop properly, as it should, your stomach will start growing, harmful substances will accumulate in your blood, abnormalities will take place. If your respiratory system gains advantage, a very bristle temper may develop in you. (...) If the nervous system is overdeveloped, people develop neurasthenia.

When nature created man, it defined what each part would be – it constructed man mathematically and geometrically. Each part must correspond to a certain magnitude and dimensions.

The very long neck is good in some respects, and bad in other. It is the same with the very short neck. Short necks are always related to the stomach system, long necks are always related to the respiratory system, with the mental activities. If your neck gets thick, then your stomach is gaining an advantage. Stomach is not neutral. When a person chooses the side of the stomach, a discord will come upon him. One must never take the side of his stomach or his lungs. But he must maintain the existing balance, to maintain harmony, which exists between lungs and stomach. Lungs must obey the brain, but stomach must obey the lungs. Any other organ in the human body must obey the stomach. Arms and legs must obey the stomach. It is the chieftain who supports them, if it stops sending food to them, legs lose their strength, arms and hands become week, feet become week.

The centre of the earth corresponds to our stomach — this is where our sympathetic nervous system is – our stomach brain. And while all your energy is focused on tour stomach, you have a positive energy in a descending order and therefore you will have to constrain yourselves. If everything is focused in your stomach, you will have no science.

As much energy comes down to the stomach, the same energy must go up to the brain.

There are three factors, which have created man: the first factor is the thought of the spirit, the second factor are the feelings of the soul and the third factor are the actions of the human mind. We say: when you serve the stomach, don't think that your mind has little participation. When you've done eating you won't be able to think – it is that simple. You must take a certain amount of food and that food must help the purification of lungs, through the juices. From the lungs it will get to the human mind, form shapes and then these shapes are to be realized. The health condition of a person, depends on his head.

If stomach has advantage over the other organs, one manifests human love.

When one seeks only the taste of things – this is the mental nature; if you are satisfied with food, the joy you feel when eating, is related to an area of the feelings. Three processes happen at the same time in one's mouth: one process is related to human mind, the other – to his feelings, and the third – to his energy, to the world of energy. Can you calculate what part of the mental energy is spent in eating? The better developed, the stronger taste is, the more mental power is spent, the bigger part pleasure takes, the bigger the part of feelings is, and if chewing takes a bigger part, it is the physical side of things.

In nature every work is important. The stomach, which deals with the lower works, first tastes the goods of life. A lot of time has to pass, before the brain gets to tasting some of these goods.

Many ask: "Why many undeserving people manage to try first the goods of life, and do it in such a great abundance?" They are in the stomach of nature. "Why don't we get to try these goods?" Don't try to get down to their level. Don't be tempted by someone else's wellbeing. They work in the stomach. While processing the food, they send it to the lungs, and from there – to the head. Your food is finer, you should wait for them to prepare it.

This triangle shows the possibilities in three rational beings, living in dependence from one another. The first is a rational being, the second is a rational being and the 3rd is a rational being. Then we say: what can the first be compared to? The first can be compared to an acid, the 1st is where the energy comes from. The second is the one which perceives. It is an alkali. The 3rd is the result, it's the salt or the law of balance. Words "balance" and "salt" are synonyms. Salt keeps the balance – things don't rot. When it comes to numbers, we should understand the law, based on which these are manifested.

Some people are nervous due to the number 3, because it is week in them. The choleric- person looses his balance. Let's say a metal oxidizes. Gold oxidizes the least, and iron oxidizes more. I say: in the old times and until now, there is science, where metals are getting precious to achieve an inner balance. Then man must study himself. We have a human nature. We have the stomach 1, lungs 2, and head 3. So one's health depends on the effect of the stomach, on the effect of the lungs and the effect of the head. In the next moment, the energies change: 3 becomes active, it becomes 4, 3 connected with 1, becomes acid; 2 connected with 3, produces the base. All of them, joined together, become salt. Then stomach, when in contact with the brain, transforms into an active number, obtains an active energy. And digestion, if the brain does not produce an urge, cannot take place properly. In order for the stomach to become active a connection with the number 3 has to be established. And then the basis will get to the sympathetic nervous system. The dynamic numbers play a role in modern psychology. One, however, has to understand this concept. If he does not understand the law, he will find himself in the position, in which he is now.

The stomach and the mind, i.e. the brain, love each other a lot. Actually, the mind always seeks stomach's opinion. If the stomach was left with the heart, to depend on it for food, it would find itself in the utmost misfortune. But because the mind always chooses good food, it sends some of it to the stomach as well. And this is good for the heart as well.

The stomach must learn the laws of the mind, it must be in harmony with the mind. There should be diplomatic relations. It should be very kind and polite towards the mind, if not – it will find itself in a difficult position. Therefore the organization starts with the stomach. This is the physical world. When we speak of all the material worlds in the universe, we mean the human stomach. You say "What is the status of the material world?" It is the same as that of your stomach. "What is the status of the spiritual world?" It is the same as that of your lungs.

The reason for the headache can be found in the small and large intestines. If they are not functioning properly, one suffers from headache.

In order to deal with the headache, one must first put his feet in hot water, and then cleanse his intestines. As soon as he alleviates his intestines and stomach, the headache will disappear.

Your head hurts, because your stomach is disordered, and the stomach is disordered, because your head is in disorder.

The vertigo is rooted in the stomach.

The pain in the head is a reflection of what happens in the stomach. Everything happens in the stomach, below the navel — this is the lower world, this is hell. You must put your small intestines in order and harmony.

Let's take modern people – sometimes they complain that their memory has weakened. You start to forget ... This is an accumulation of the so-called "lactic acid". Many times, when lactic acid accumulates in the brain, the brain becomes indolent, it can't work, there's not enough electricity. Then the lactic acid descends down to the solar plexus the solar plexus. This is when the magnetic field of a person is disturbed, - you start being indisposed, feeling bad. No medicines can help. There are two things that will help a nervous disease clean food, well-chewed food. When you eat, you must think of nothing else. You must be grateful for being able to eat

In order to recover your memory, you must relieve your mind of all the accumulated lactic acid. How do you do that? By cleansing the brain, by cleansing all the blood in the entire body. This is achieved by changing the food, with pure thoughts, pure feelings and deeds.

The headache occurs always when heart is indisposed. When the mind is indisposed, the stomach suffers. The head is indisposed, but the stomach suffers. The heart is indisposed, but the head suffers.

What would you do about the headache, how would you do that exercise? The reason about the pain in your head is somewhere in your stomach. There the capillaries of the blood-vessels fail to perform properly, and – as a result – the sympathetic nervous system of the stomach, fails to function properly. And the sympathetic nervous system delivers more strength, more moisture to the digestion. The most important functions in the body are performed by the sympathetic nervous system.

The stomach-ache shows that the energy in the stomach must be transformed from positive to negative. The headache shows that the energy in the head, which is positive, must be transformed into negative, compared to all the other energies. Your mind must be occupied by higher activities.

There are three processes and one has to master them all. The process of eating is a physical process, the process of sensing and the process of speaking. If the process of eating is not correct in you, your speaking will also be incorrect. If the process of eating is correct, speaking will also be correct. Because there is a parallel between the stomach and the brain, they are alike. The same way the stomach is demanding, the brain is also demanding. They are the opposite poles in life. Because the stomach is connected to the stomach brain, which deals with all the bodily functions, they all join in it.

When the stomach brain and the stomach are not functioning properly, man suffers from headache. When the brain isn't working well, your stomach aches. In order to heal the headache, you must first correct the disturbed relations of the front part of the brain and its rear part. If the front part is not working properly, you suffer from headache. And the stomach is disturbed, due to the rear part of the brain. If that part of the brain gets wormer than the front part, if the temperature of that part increases by one tenth of the degree, a sickness will come upon you. If one gets sick with grief over a beloved one, and because the centre of love is in the back, love increases the temperature. Why one gets sick? One thinks of his or her beloved one, wants to have her or him constantly by one's side. Nature will never let you to appropriate anything it has given to you. It gives you something to use, but not to appropriate – it always counteracts in such event. If you want to take possession of what has been given to you, you will only cause yourself some kind of a sickness. You have the right to love, but you have no right to appropriate. You have the right to eat, but you don't have the right to overeat. You have the right to cry, but you don't have the right to squall, to yell, to snap

When you are anxious, raise your hands in the air and then put them down. Then you say to your stomach: "Listen, buddy, let the brain stay up and you – down; send it some material, to make it work". In general – where there is headache, the stomach suffers as well, and vice versa. This shows that the law is always true — there is a strong connection between the stomach and the head.

When the pores are open, the stomach acts well, correctly. The pores are channel, through which nature's energy flows into the body. The healthy and normal digestive system ensures a normal, and thus – properly working respiratory system.

If there is no harmony between you sympathetic nervous system and your brain, if the stomach system produces more heat than necessary, you will find yourself in a conflict. If the brain system produces more cold, if the brain system is overdeveloped, people become dry. The skin gets dry, it has no moisture. You must change the condition immediately. What are you supposed to do? You should drink more water – a litre, litre and a half, or even two litres. You must drink not more than two and a half litres of water in a day. Water is a good conductor of electricity and magnetism. You say: "I can't do without water". Water is necessary not only to cleanse the body, but to ensure the functioning of the sympathetic nervous system.

When a person loses water, he dries out. When there is too much water he becomes obese. You can't think if you don't have an excellent nervous system, which transfers the mental vibrations. If your sympathetic nervous system is not well developed, so that you have enough water, things will be fruitless — the heart cannot function. In order for your mind to function, the brain system must be developed. In order for the heart to function, for you to have noble feelings, your sympathetic nervous system has to be developed. For you not to be irritable, not to get angry, your liver and gall-bladder must work properly. Some people are choleric, real spitfire – this means their liver is disordered. The digestion of some people is not working properly – this means their sympathetic nervous system is not fine.

The external side of the spiritual life is the warmth that is produced, the light, the so-called thoughts and feelings of a person. This is the connection. Feelings are connected with one's stomach, thoughts are connected with one's blood circulation.

At times you feel a heaviness in your stomach, but you don't know the reason for that. If you are aware of the functions of the sympathetic nervous system, you will know that this heaviness, this indisposition in the stomach area, is related to your feelings, to the sympathetic nervous system. You have eaten food, the vibrations of which do not correspond to those of your sympathetic nervous system, and this results in a disharmony. When this ailing condition somehow passes, you start feeling mentally indisposed. So the pain has moved to your head, to your temples, where you feel a great pressure. That is why one has to be careful about what he eats, to know what kind of food his body needs.

Warmth comes through taking food. Warmth carries life. The continuation of life depends on the warmth, on the warm heart.

IN order for the nutrition to be proper, heart's pulse must be in harmony with the pulse of nature. The improper pulse is most often the result of improper digestion.

During digestion it is not enough to produce nutritional juices, these have to be properly oxidized, in order to give the blood its red color. Pure blood contains all the vital elements, as well as kinetic and potential energy, which are the reasons for the formation of thought. Within the blood circulation there is a back flow of blood, which can and return to the spiritual body of a man. Blood-flow is not only a physical, but also a spiritual process. By physical process we mean only this, which is visible and can be put to test. There are things, which can't be seen with an unarmed eye, and cannot be put to test.

Through food a man consumes the external materials for building not only his body, but also his soul.

At first you must relieve the stomach, relieve the stomach system. Often you overload the stomach, you don't give it any freedom, you don't let it rest. You must relieve the stomach, to give it only as much work, as it is comfortable with. These cells, which form the stomach, are an entire nation, like the Bulgarians. Give them their freedom so that they can do their job. The work they do should be pleasant to them, don't make them slaves. As soon as stomach's cells become slaves, you stop being a free person. After that you must release your lungs. Sometimes you make them very indolent. Lungs' indolence produces various conditions. A person, once he becomes indolent, becomes very demanding, he always wants a soft chair, wants to lie down comfortably, to have a soft bed, comfortable shoes, to have an exquisite house, not to have anything in his way and be served by everybody.

Sensitiveness depends to a great degree on stomach's condition. You can't have normal feelings, if your stomach doesn't function well. By "potbelly" I mean something unreasonable, disordered eating, gluttony. If you don't eat reasonably, you won't have reasonable feelings either.

When one is too much worried, the worries produce disturbance first in his stomach system.

When a person does not think and feel right, his digestion does not work properly, venous blood, carrying all the diseases, is formed. Another situation: when a person does not think and feel right, he does not breathe well. When a person does not think and feel right, his nervous system, his brain system and sympathetic nervous system do not function properly and then neurasthenia. So your thought is only proper when your thoughts and feelings are right and only when they improve your digestion. Your thoughts and feelings are only right, when they improve your respiratory system. Your thoughts and feelings are only right, when they improve your brain system and sympathetic nervous system. If there is a conflict in these three areas, your thoughts and feelings are not right.

The tongue can be bribed, to be lied to, but the stomach — never! It says: "Hey Mister, this thing has to go out. I can't process it. If you put that a second time, I will throw it out again. You must know that I don't do such things." There are three things in life, which one has to listen to, and which he must believe: he must listen to his stomach, what kind of food it wants. Not to ask his taste, but to listen to his stomach. The second thing, which one must listen to, are the lungs. He must ask them what kind of air do they want. And finally, he must ask his brain, what kind of food he should take.

We are a conglomerate, a common organism, formed by millions, billions of small souls, living together, at one place. Each of you is a whole country. Modern people must learn to speak with their heads, with their stomach, until they know all the cells.

Some ask: "Why do some people have weak lungs?" Because they don't breathe. "Why some people's stomach is weak?" Because they don't practice their mouths. A man who does not know how to speak, will always have a weak stomach. And if a man does not know how to look, his brain would be weak. There are three things: you must look, so that your brain is healthy, you must breathe so that your chest is healthy, and you must speak, so that your stomach is healthy. These are basic things.

Develop your hearing so that you catch good sounds. Develop your vision, so that you see the best of beauties! Develop your smell so that you get the best fragrance! Develop your taste, so that what you eat, what you do, you should thank god for his infinite love for you.

God wants us to live long and happy lives, and we have put ourselves in slavery through the diseases. In order to get well, you must take not of the following: believe that light has an absolute power to heal all diseases, believe that air has an absolute power to heal all diseases, believe that water has an absolute power to heal all diseases, believe that food has an absolute power to heal all diseases, because of God's presence in them.

"Lord, enlighten the head that You have given to me, so that I can learn to work!" After that put your hands on your lungs for 10 minutes and pray for them. Then put your hands on your belly. The word "belly" does not mean stomach, but those digestive organs, which we refer to as stomach. Pray for 10 minutes for you to know how to eat. To know how food is digested, to be thankful about that food, because the basis of life is put in the stomach. If you have a good basis, put in the stomach, your entire life will be good. If you have building materials in your lungs, your entire life will be good. You must have a roof, a house well done. After that the spirit and soul can enter that house and everything would be calm.

THE FALL OF MAN

Had people lived at the pole, I can't say what kind of culture they would have. It is very difficult to be vegetarian there, all beings at the pole are carnivorous. Man does not live under the most favourable conditions. Is it is said in the Bible – he was created on the equator, where there is an abundance of fruit, and he can be a vegetarian.

It was a time, when the Earth resembled a paradise, the vegetation was so abundant, there were thousands and millions of fruits and people lived only on fruit, but then an ice age started, which was due to certain physical reasons. Then these fruitfulness of the Earth decreased and, as a result, people started eating meat, and killing not only animals, but started slaughtering and eating each other.

It was a time, when the sons cooked their fathers and mothers. They didn't bury them. Before the father dies – one would cook and eat him. And eat one's mother. Joseph Flavius tells about the siege of Jerusalem, when mothers grilled and ate their children. All types of things happened!

If a person, after eating meat, is healthy – let him eat. If one, after eating vegetarian food, gets sick let him eat meat. Let him pay for the future. If one, after eating vegetarian food is healthy – let him eat. For thousands of years people ate not only animals, but other people too. Back in the old days, when they fought and killed each other, people used to consume their enemies. They ate everybody they killed. We have managed to release ourselves from a great evil – eating human flesh. It is so differentiated that it brings in a great infection.

The apple, mentioned in the Bible, is the unnatural food, which man started eating. And the fall of man started with flesh-eating. Even the fall of angels is also due to flesh-eating, and flesh-eating is the result of the personal egoism of man, who overlooks the interests of animals. A man, who is flesh-eating, may commit any other crime.

I understand if you say man did some mistakes, but to claim that man is incorrigible – this is a false conclusion. There a numerous facts and evidences that man sinned and continues to sin, to commit crimes. But what data do you have that man is incorrigible? To correct and understand his mistakes – this is a privilege given only to man. This privilege distinguishes him from all other animals. On the path of his descend on Earth, man has deviated from the correct direction of his movement, and – as a result – he did many mistakes and committed many crimes. If it is not so, how can you explain the origin of flesh-eating animals? How were fish and some carnivorous birds created? All animals, in general, are phases, through which man has passed within the process of his development. When he starts to ascend, man will acknowledge his mistakes and start to correct them.

Which was the driving cause for some angels to leave heaven – the place of eternal bliss and purity, the place of joy and merriment – and come to the Earth among the sinful sons of man? Who made them leave heaven and lose their purity? They have descended from that glory and come to the Earth among people in the form of beasts, to do mischief. At a time in the distant past, the flesh-eating animals were angels, which are now here among us as animals, doing mischief to the people. At first they were peaceable like sheep, but when they descended on Earth in the form of tigers, wolves, lions, they started attacking and eating the herbivorous animals.

Flesh-eating was initiated by the fallen spirits; it came to the world when the connection with Love was interrupted.

Not to eat meat means that we don't pleasure ourselves. To pleasure ourselves means to commit a sin, i.e. to eat food, for which our bodies are not ready. Should we eat such food, it becomes a poison. The meat food is poison. Meat symbolizes the "tree of the knowledge of good and evil".

The Lord created animals for very different reasons – not to be eaten by man, making them serve the man, but not to be slaughtered by him. Wheat, corn, maze, rye, grains and fruits were meant by God as food. After the fall of man people became flesh-eating.

By knowing good and evil man assumed the idea of flesh-eating, and after that – of murder. When eating meat you can't help but kill.

Nature only records two things: good and evil. They go along together. The herbivorous animals record good, carnivorous – record evil. And it is the same with people.

I believe evil is flesh-eating, and good is fruit-feeding, and not vegetarianism. Meat, in the astral worlds, is a symbol of evil, and when they want to show you that your deeds are evil, they will give you meat as food. When you dream that you are given meat, this means that you are on an unnatural path. When I speak of man, I mean the spiritual man, because two beings live in the body together. I speak of the rational being. Two beings live together now, and their lives do not converge and therefore between these two beings and the Divine Man there is a fight, because their lives are incompatible.

The flesh is flesh-eating, and the spirit – fruit-feeding. Everybody, in whom the flesh is strong, is flesh-eating. Everybody, in whom the spirit has taken advantage, are fruit-feeding. Flesh-eating is due to the strong human flesh, and that is why they go together. (…) This is in the law of flesh.

The culture in the world goes in two ways: there is a culture of good and there is a culture of evil. There are people, who study culture of good, and others, who study the culture of evil. How do they differ? Take a wolf for example – he studies the culture of evil years and years – he knows how to catch a sheep, how to kill it. A fox knows how to catch a chicken, how to kill it. That wolf has practiced a long time. When did he first think of catching and eating a sheep? What was the cause for that? Some say that flesh-eating animals learned to eat meat during the ice age, because the plantation was scarce. These are just speculations. Why the white blood-cells in the human body, devour a germ, as soon as it enters the body? These white blood cells are like sentries. They catch the enemies, entering the human blood, and eat them. You may say this is a instinct. Instincts are rational urges in nature. What makes a wolf eat sheep, or what makes sheep eat grass? There is something in nature, which makes them do that. Therefore nature has two drives. Haven't many of you eaten grilled chickens – even if it was 25-30 years ago, when you were kids? You sat with your mothers, while she killed the chicken, and waited for her to cook its liver. What urged you to eat that? How did it occur to you that liver is to be eaten? It would never occur to an angel, to eat chicken's liver, when it is killed.

If everything was created to be eaten, then why don't you kill a wolf, or a spider, or a bear and eat it? Why do you make a difference? Moses, in a code, forbade his people to eat pork, because pig's hoof is cloven. Rabbits must not be eaten either – they also have something cloven.

What brought sin into the world? The deviation, fragmentation, difference in shapes, the presence of sexes, the difference in people's desires, the difference in people's thoughts and feelings. All the collisions of these forces brought sin into the world – nothing more. Because, when some ask, how did sin enter the world, here's what I say: plant a garden and you will see how sin entered the world. Those children, who are considered very upright, as soon as they pass by a garden, planted with fine fruit, will always be tempted. Right, and what is better now: to have orchards and sustain some thefts, or not to have orchards and not to suffer any thefts? Life to exist, along with death, or life not to exist, there being no death either?

Animals have been stealing for a long time. It is an animal condition. Before people started stealing, wolves had been stealing and eaten sheep for a long time, spires had been stealing and eating flies for a long time. In theft there is already an atavist work of the animal kingdom.

All the flesh-eating animals are thieves. Theft was formed by the flesh-eating animals – the foxes, wolves, bears, snakes, spiders. All the flesh-eating animals are the fathers of theft. You steal they are your fathers, from whom you learned theft. All the good things we've learned from the herbivorous animals. The herbivorous animals are virtuous. For me there are two things, which are impossible: a sheep can't eat a wolf, and a wolf can't graze down a field. There are two possible things: a wolf can eat a sheep and a sheep can graze down a field. If the field is grazed down, it's sheep's fault. If sheep is eaten, it's wolf's fault. Who ate it? The wolf. Who grazed down the field? The sheep. The sheep is more practical, it bites off the grass and lets it grow again. Here's what I say: bring those who are guilty. Sheep's case will be referred to the court of peace, while wolf's case is a criminal one.

Moses put down a law that man must not lie, for lie is not an invention of man. Then he says: "Do not kill!" It is once again an animal condition —

murder was created by the carnivorous animals. You say one is a hero – he killed – this is an animal condition.

In eating we have a process of destruction. You take an apple and you destroy it. Here's what I say: what harmony can be created in a world, where things are constantly destroyed? The fish, when it came upon this issue, in order not to destroy when eating, it swallows food whole. It swallows food whole through its mouth, but when the food enters fish's stomach, it is chewed by it.

Most fish in the sea are carnivorous. All of them eat each other. Very few fish, and most of them – of higher level, are vegetarian. Fishes devour each other. The larger fish devours the smaller one, an even bigger fish devours the first one, yet another bigger fish devours all three. When you catch a big fish and open its belly, you will see that it has devoured another fish, which, on its part, has devoured an even smaller fish. The largest fish has devoured all three.

How can you solve this issue, tell me that! The small fish, which has devoured an even smaller one, thinks it has established well its life. And then another fish comes and eats it. This second fish now thinks that its life goes well, but then the largest fish comes and eats them both, thinking that it's life is great. And finally man comes with his net, catches the largest fish, takes it out of the water, opens up its belly, takes the two smaller fishes and keeps the largest. The small fishes are not good to him, so he throws them out and keeps the largest, believing that it does him good.

The herbivorous animals have their molars developed. In those, who eat meat, the front and canine teeth are very well developed. Now you have both types. You will look at the teeth — they show what different people eat.

How come eagle's beak is curved? It is to help it tear away meat, when hitting. Then his feet assumed a shape, conforming to its jaw – the claws on its feet are with the same shape.

In the predators, who want to grab — their upper beak is bent inwards, so that they can catch and hold their prey. Those birds, which only live on grains, don't have curved beaks – see the pigeon for example. Predators are great pessimists. Those who live on grains, like the pigeon, have not pessimism in them at all. And those of you, who are pessimists – you are predators. Whatever you say to such a person, he looks at everything with disbelief.

The pigeon – from the beginning of ages – is the only bird, who hasn't been tempted by meat. Despite all difficulties through which the pigeon has gone, he has had the nobleness to remain vegetarian. He has never said: "The living conditions are difficult and I must eat some meat". On the contrary – he says: "Whatever the living conditions are, I will overcome them. Because God is ration, I will be rational too, I will eat grains and nothing else!"

How does the sheep and how does the wolf eat? You haven't observed that. Sometime, when you have time enough, look at how wolves and sheep eat. Look at how do vegetarians eat, and how do flesh-eating persons eat. And what will you see, what is the difference in eating? How does the flesh-eating person hold his fork and knife? The same way the vegetarian holds them. But there is a significant difference. Flesh-eating people are more dexterous in eating. There is a certain dexterity in them. All those who live on meat, are a little impatient. They are a little choleric. This habit has even remained in vegetarians. And if a vegetarian is irritable, this means that he has just started eating vegetarian food. Whoever was born vegetarian, is a little calmer, does not hurry.

Flesh-eating animals are greedy, they gulp down their food, the herbivorous collect food and then, when they sit down – they regurgitate their food and start chewing it, as when you make sops or tarhana.

The herbivorous biter off their food-, then swallow it, and ruminate — they have double stomachs.

Why do animals ruminate? Rumination is a method of nature. In order for a being to be able to transform from one state to another, it must ruminate. And, when we say that we must transform from one state to another, this is, because we are in a constant pressure, thought has accumulated and it is to be assimilated, by separating the useful from the useless, and then you get a processed material.

Flesh-eating animals are very perspicacious, cunning, they have a strategy. Their moral is based on their pleasure, this is so with the wolf, the bear, the lion – all these carnivorous animals. If there is no pleasure, it's not moral. The vegetarian food, on the other hand, will strengthen even more the nervous system, create a sturdier nervous system. A resistant, more enduring body is formed. All herbivorous animals are more enduring.

In all flesh-eating animals, the sense of self-preservation is well developed. Among the herbivorous animals – this feeling is not developed so well. That is why they don't get so angry. For example, if an ox gets angry, it can gauge you, but first it would press you down to the ground with his horns. If a lion, tiger or a wolf attacks you, it would tear off whatever he gets. A herbivorous animal would never do that.

There are a number of reasons for people to be meat-eating or vegetarian. Meat-eating and vegetarianism do not solve the social issues in the world. These are only the preparatory phases for many or few virtues. The herbivorous animals have a softer mature than the flesh-eating. If a bull or another herbivorous animal catches you, it can kick you or gouge you with its horns, but never tear you apart. If a flesh-eating animal catches you, however, it can tear you to pieces. This is their nature. The herbivorous animals are soft, and the flesh-eating – fierce. The herbivorous animals are negative by nature, and the carnivorous   positive.

There is not a single meek carnivorous animal, all of them are like wasps. Wasps are carnivorous. If you observe the movement of a bee and the movement of a wasp – you will notice that they differ greatly. In the movement of the bee there is nobleness, and in the flight of the wasp there is something pirate. While it is flying, it is irritable. If you disturb it, it will sting you right away.

Wolf's head is wider, and sheep's – longer and narrower. The heads of all peaceful creatures, of most mammals of softer nature, are narrow? When the peaceful creatures think more, they are more active, more agile. A flesh-eating animal loves running. The herbivorous animals run to save their lives, and, otherwise, the movement is always within them. Others at first run, then their running slows down and they stop. Those with wide heads, have a hidden energy and that hidden energy in the carnivorous animals, is the reason for their many quarrels over food. There are no quarrels over food among herbivorous animals. The quarrels among herbivorous animals are over love: two rams fight, because of love affairs – they bang their heads. Here's what I say now: why do they fight, what is the reason for their fighting over food? So if fight over food, you are also among the flesh-eating animals.

Humans are fruit-eaters, according to their body structure. Meat is stronger, but more harmful food. It contains more poisons and makes a man rude and cruel.

People get sick, degenerate and die, because they are meat-eaters.

According to the food--, they use, people are divided into vegetarians and meat-eaters. There are vegetarians from birth, but there are also vegetarians, who have been using plant food for 10-20 years. When we talk about vegetarians and compare them to the meat-eaters, we mean the first category. The heads of the vegetarians--, compared to those of the meat-eaters-- are longer and narrower, while that of the meat-eaters-- is wider and shorter. The heads of the meat-eaters-- in general, are wider around the ears. This shows that the destructive powers are well developed in them. Food-- affects both the physical and the spiritual and mental lives of people.

Man thinks that by eating meat, he will be healthier. This is not so. Meat-eating animals are more energetic, but the herbivorous are stronger. Is a tiger stronger than an elephant? What work can an ox do, and what – a wolf?

You may say that meat is better, stronger. If it is about strength, there are no stronger than the herbivorous animals. Is there a stronger animal than the elephant? He can fight everybody.

What would a man acquire, by eating meat? He will become stronger. But eating plant food he will become cleaner. Meat-eating animals are stronger, crueller, more predatory. If you are a wolf, you eat meat. If you are a sheep, you eat grass. The desires of the wolf are desires of the Black Lodge, and the desires of the sheep are desires of the White Lodge.

Plant food gives patience.

Whoever has a strong will, he is meek and humble. You may say that you don't want to be meek as a sheep. A sheep is not meek. It has a softness, and not meekness in it. The sheep has made enormous efforts, before it became a sheep. Once it was a wolf and then it became a sheep. Whoever wants to acquire softness, love, should eat mutton. As soon as he obtains these qualities, he no longer needs such meat.

The vegetarian food enhances the nervous system. A strong, more robust body is formed.

Vegetarianism means meekness.

The loveless people are meat-eaters. The choleric- people are always sick. Is there a patient sick person? Everything seems wrong and dark to him, and he claims that his conditions are poor. Such a person better becomes a vegetarian, because plant food gives patience.

Meat food is nervous and fruit-food is a conductor of magnetism.

A person, who eats vegetarian food, becomes braver. The centre of conscience is above the centre of fear. Once a man develops his conscience, it takes the extra energy from fear and transforms it into justice.

The new life, which is now being brought in, must have a very different basis. I am not talking against the current life. You will live through this current life, as it is. When it comes to the old life – whoever eats meat – let him eat meat, whoever eats grass – let him eat grass, whoever drinks wine, let him drink wine. Whoever drinks water – let him drink water. Whoever eats fruits – let him eat fruits. Whatever one has learned – let him do that and nothing more. Don't teach people new things. Why should you try teaching sheep to eat meat and wolves to graze grass? Don't try to settle these issues. If you are angry, you should know that such ill feelings are due to the meat-eating animals in us. If you are quiet and calm, this condition is due to the herbivorous animals in us. These are two different conditions. When you think, people in you have the word. When you are good, don't think that this goodness is your own achievement — goodness is available to all mankind. Goodness is a great gift, the Lord has given the entire mankind. Therefore, one you are good, you benefit from that great gift.

Whatever one does – this is for his future. Let me tell you what heaven is. You have already created your heaven. You think of going to the other world, and be welcomed there. But at least 200 chickens will appear before you, demanding their lives. 300 calves will appear, to demand parts of their legs, ribs, lungs that you have eaten. Ducks will also come, then snails, mussels… After that the trees that you have cut down, the leaves, flowers you have picked – everything will demand their lives and yell at you. What will you do? The Lord will send you to satisfy them. You must return the lives to all the flowers, trees, chickens etc. After this is done and your debt is repaid, the Lord will summon you and ask: "How do you want to live?" You will learn your lesson and then, when you go to God, you will say: "I have learned my lesson – the next time you send me to the Earth, I will live, as You live ".

When you eat meat, you must sign contracts with these animals, for one day you will be sent the bill for all the meat you have eaten. You will definitely pay! You'll be told that there is a proper book-keeping in nature and you'll be asked why have you eaten meat? You must prove that scientifically.

Everybody will be judged. Who, among you, has not eaten 100

chickens? Who has not eaten 100 lambs? Who has not eaten 100 fishes? You would say: "Christ also roasted these". I understand things in a different way. Don't cook the fish that you don't love. Cook those fishes that you love. When you eat a cooked fish, which you don't love, you would inflict on it the greatest evil, which you can't even imagine.

What would, however, happen to the one who has eaten 100 chickens? He will be put among those 100, right when they are being killed, and he will feel their condition. This will happen one hundred times, and this is a horrible thing. And finally, people will become vegetarians, because they will refuse to eat meat in an internal manner.

When I speak about people's feeding habits, I don't judge them, but I say that as many chickens or turkeys one has eaten throughout his life, that many chickens and turkeys he shall serve. As many lambs he has eaten – that many lambs he will serve. This is the law of nature. The disturbed balance has to be restored. Therefore, you will be free to eat whatever food you want, but you will know that all that will be paid through being in service.

The chicken that you eat will loose nothing, it will only win, but you will loose. In this respect, the hermitic philosophy maintains the following view: All the chickens you have eaten, all the lambs and fishes, you have eaten, when these chickens, lambs, fishes become people, you may be in the position of an angel, and the Lord will send you to help and serve them on the Earth. He will say to you: "They used to sustain your life, and now it is your turn to serve them ". They will wonder why does that angel help and love them. The angel will say: "I am obliged to you". You will go along the law of obligations.

You must know that one day you will give all the mammals, all the birds, which you have eaten, all the necessary conditions to return to the Earth. You will be the reason for them to return to the Earth and progress. Not just that, but the Lord will send you to serve them. God sends an angel to a sinful person, to serve him. He is tied down. You will serve your ox, which now ploughs for you. You will pat it and won't goad it. These things are still not understood by the man. When the Providence comes to put you in harness, then things will be clear. Think of that time! So, you'll come back to help all creatures, to which you are indebted.

Meat-eating animals have high esteem of themselves; they believe that mentally they are positioned higher than the herbivorous. He herbivorous animals, are of higher culture, in terms of their hearts, than the meat-eating.

Therefore there are two cultures among animals: the culture of the mind and the culture of the heart. The herbivorous animals represent the culture of the heart and that is why they are better – they have a clean, noble heart. Meat-eating animals are cleverer, but they are not better in their hearts. And now you, as rational people, can connect both principles – those of the lion and the sheep, and say: "We will be clever as the lion and good as the sheep. We will tear down evil, like the lion and save the grass, like the sheep, and give room for the goodness in us to grow."

FOOD - WAY OF LIFE

There are several sources for man's vital forces —food-, air, water and light. Other sources are his thought, feelings and deeds. Each one uses such food, which corresponds to his development. Ordinary people eat in an ordinary way – they take the food- and chew it. The adepts only eat air. And some of them only consume air once a month, others – once a year, and the most advanced – once in their entire lives. They differ from ordinary people in processing their food a long time. There are adepts, who live only on light.

Most saints and adepts eat food, knowing how to draw out their nutritional juices. All the creatures, which have completed their development, use food which is more ethereal than fruit. This makes them eternal. Eating brings in death, through the discharge of the microbes.

Each item of food must correspond the development of a person. According to the degree of his mental and spiritual development, some only eat meat, others – plant food, and yet another – fruit. It is important for a person to know how to eat.. When it comes to the evolution of the soul, one will only eat fruit.

The food-, people consume define if they are going to be smart or stupid. This depends not only on you, but also on your parents, on your grandparents and predecessors. It depends also greatly on food-, which your mothers and fathers had eaten, as well as the food of your predecessors. This is a whole science.

The way one eats, defines what kind of a person he is mentally and spiritually. The process of eating is a sacred act, which should be treated with all due seriousness.

God never helps people, who do not know how to eat, how to breathe or how to think.

Eating is a force, which can bring you closer to God.

The simplest reaching, which you may apply even now, is the teaching of proper eating. I advise all of you to get down to the teaching of nutrition, and not to think that you already have your pass to heaven.

If people want to be saved, they must start from the food. The new generation must be created out of fine matter.

One brings such elements to his blood, as the food he eats. Knowing that, he must keep his blood clean, because health depends on it, as does his mental condition.

The eating habits and the life one lives, may provide information on how many years his car, i.e. his body will serve him. This also depends on one's reasonableness. One who does not live reasonably is destined to a premature aging; when one gets old, his leg get weak and fail him. Such a person is thus dependant on other people and often becomes a toy in their hands.

Education must start from eating. Eating is a Divine process. Then entire mistake of eve was that she did not know how to eat. She did not listen to the Lord, but listened to others, who advised her to eat the fruits of the forbidden tree. If you eat what s suggested by people, there will always be indisposition and ill mood. There is an internal feeling in everybody, which tells them what to eat – you should listen to that.

Improper eating harms the good relations between people.

The life which we may spend on Earth will be defined, according to the food-- of our mind, of our heart and of our bodies. All the diseases are born of our minds and our hearts. The stomach and soul get sick, because we give them bad food. If there is not enough light in one's mind, neurasthenia-- is already at the threshold.

When you study life, study first those elements, which sustain it. These are the strongest desires – i.e. breathing and eating. Knowing the main desires of a person, you can determine his secondary desires.

If an angel eats human food, he will become a human, and loose his angelic qualities.

When in one's life there are a series of failures, accompanied by series of illnesses, suffering, loss of money, including among his relatives etc. People start dying in this family and if you trace the lives of the entire family, of the entire kin, you will see that the reason for the death is due to the improper eating. All the miseries are due to improper eating. Whoever does not believe that, should – when misery falls upon him – check and see what food had he been eating and continues to eat. This is the only way he can be convinced of the truth in my words. In this respect nature has been very careful. It has created an abundance of food for everybody, and also created suitable food for all different living conditions. If you want to develop the mind, heart or will, you will have to use the respective food for them. If you want to be an artist, a painter or a musician, or a scientists, you must choose the suitable food. Through food only you will be able to achieve what you want.

If modern science wants to change the nature of man, it must start by selecting the food. For example, if you live for one month only on cherries, one month only on apples, one month only on plums, a month or two only on potatoes, only on wheat or barley or only on rye, or rice, or peas, or beans, or kohlrabi, or cabbage, if you eat only grapes for one month, you will see what effect this will have. All these foods have different effects. Each fruit has specific qualities, which are transferred to man. So, here's what I say: we get acquainted with the fruit-trees, with fruit and acquire the respective qualities, which they have. We process that material of the plant kingdom. They are better at capturing the energies, coming from the sun and process them for people.

Artists tried – one they had to play the part of the perfect love – to eat mutton for a long time, because this meat is conductive to such feelings.

Out philosophy depends on eating. Your philosophic belief, your religious belief depend on eating, your art depends on food-. If this food is not pure, you won't have a bright mind, if that food is not pure, you won't see anything around you. An artist with a poisoned blood cannot see and paint good pictures; if a musician's blood is poisoned, he cannot play properly; a mother with a poisoned blood, cannot raise her children; a teacher with a poisoned blood cannot educate children.

In order to understand which food is healthier, let's make the following experiment: we will impose a regime on a person - for three months we will feed him only pork and let him drink half a litre of wine three times a day. Another person will love on a fruit regime — for two months he will eat exclusively fruit and drink clean, hot water. During the experiment we will observe both, and see what their relations with their relatives and the other people around them are.

Food-, coming from above, gives life. The life, descending from heaven, aims at transforming the current people. Man cannot be transformed in any way, if he does not change his food. Until then, while the wolf eats meat, he will remain a wolf. Food-- defines character. In order for the criminal to be corrected, he should be given suitable food. If you give a criminal only wheat for three years, you will see how he shall change.

The happiness of a person depends on his eating. If he knows how to eat, he will be happy.

If you observe a man, while he is eating, you will know what will happen. You will know the results from the eating. Sometimes, when somebody comes to me, I divinate otherwise. I have a science, which I keep to myself. Sometimes I, wanting to find out what a person is, I give him lunch than I have the precise data, where everything is predetermined. And sometimes I give lunch to myself and observe myself, and again I know what will I do. But teach this art to nobody. This is something that cannot be conveyed. So I say: if you know how to eat, everything in this world depends on that.

The good fortune in any area generally depends on man's eating. Look at how somebody is eating and you will see if he will become smart, a scientists, if he will be good, well-spoken, a musician. Eating can produce anything. When you see somebody eating 4-5 times, you can tell what will become of him.

Depending on what food you eat, this is what you will become. This law is correct in both the physical and the spiritual world. Animal or human blood, shed through violence, cannot but bring bad consequences for man. This is a strict and stern law of nature.

Just observe what food one eats. You don't have to know his nature. It is enough to know what kind of food he eats. When you see what kind of food he eats, you will know what his character is. You say: "How is this possible?" Just see what food does the wolf or spider, or the snake eat, and you will see what their character is. What does the sheep eat? Grass. So food has created the wolf, food has created the snake, food has created sheep's character etc.

Through food you will understand the character. The wolf, which eats meat, has a different character, from that of the sheep, which eats plants. People who eat regular food, have one character, and those who eat the Divine Food, have another character.

The wolf cannot commit a crime in one case, and in another the wolf can commit a crime. The wolf can commit a crime – he can eat a wolf; the wolf cannot eat a wolf. The sheep can graze down a field. A wolf can never graze down a field. It is all about the capabilities. If the wolf devours a sheep – whose fault it is – wolf's or sheep's? It is sheep's. What does the sheep do up there in the mountains with the wolf? If the sheep grazes down a field, is it sheep's or field's fault? It is field's. What does the field do near the sheep? So the law here is the same. The sheep, which stands still is eaten by the wolf. The field, which stands still, is grazed down by the sheep.

Evil is not in eating. When a certain food is being forbidden, this is done in order to avoid any suffering of the being, using that food.

All the evil, suffered by people, is due to the fact that they eat the apples, without sawing their seeds. They milk the cow, without taking care of it. They milk it, give it some straw and on Sunday they give it some grain – they use the cow. Nature never likes mere use. Here's what I say: woe to those who use their neighbours! (...) Woe to them. Blessed are those who do not use.

Do you think a wolf is just to a sheep, by catching and tearing it to pieces? If you ask why it tears the sheep to pieces, the wolf would say: "This is a pastry, made for me, to try it ". The wolf would reply about the sheep, the same way you would about the pastry. When you tear apart a pastry, you just say: "It is done for me", and you put no life at all in the pastry. The wolf never thinks that there is a soul in the sheep, and it suffers — the wolf sees it as a pastry. Whether the wolf thinks like that or not – this is a matter of comparison, I am just making a comparison – you can make a comparison as well – there is similarity. If the wolf could grasp that the sheep suffers, and that one day it shall suffer as well, it would never do such a thing. It considers that a necessity – it must eat the sheep in that given case.

We, modern people too justify our deeds the same way. When we slaughter a sheep and say: "This is a necessity for us ". There is no divine law, which forbids that. In nature there is no law, which says what should be eaten. Eating meet for us is an arbitrary act.

The reflection of the angels are the tetrapods — cows, oxen etc. They are the reflection of angels on earth. Who are the daughters? The sons and daughters are here, among us. How do you treat the sons and daughters? You say: "This is a cow, ox, sheep" etc. Then what do you understand of life? This is yourselves! These are your brothers and sisters, which sacrifice themselves for your life. They die every day. You butcher them, eat them, take their milk and butter and settle a great question: what is God.

More than 35 million animals die in an ear, not of natural death, but because they are killed by people. The least number of animals are killed in India. Their religion maintains that animals, and especially mammals, must not be killed. The greatest number of cattle is in India. There they live to very old age and are respected like old people. When they die, these animals are buried. While they are alive, only their milk and wool is used, but never their meet, because they do not use meet. People in Europe eat a lot of meet.

A lot of meet is eaten abroad. In America they butcher about 35—40 million pigs every year. There have never been such an onslaught of mammals as now, and that is why there is an abnormal condition in the organic world. Animals have developed the stomach system of people.

Seventy-five percent of the current sufferings of people are due to that indiscriminate killing of mammals, of animals, which form cataclysms in the mental world, a great quake. The fact that the nervous system is so shaken, is due to the indiscriminate killing of animals by the white race - this race not only kills animals, but also conserves them. They just stay and rot for years.

The outrageous slaughtering of animals for food produces a great turmoil in the astral world, the entire atmosphere is disturbed, and we want to be healthy in this situation! For this injustice – for taking their lives, we will suffer a long time.

I would like those claim that animals should be butchered, to show me a single healthy person! Of there is none – let them prove what the reasons are for people not to be healthy. We, cultural people, think that these creatures are our slaves. If we are the masters of the world, let us rule over sicknesses. We cannot rule over sicknesses, poverty, indigence, or earthquakes either.

Fear and anger give birth to a terrible poison. I am against meat-eating, because when animals are butchered, when their lives are taken, fear and hatred arise in them, and then one of the most dangerous poisons is born, that poison has poisoned the entire white race. All the nervousness, which is observed among men, is due to the slaughtering of mammals. These are millions of creatures, which – when they enter the astral world – they disturb the entire atmosphere, and yet we want to be healthy. All the sicknesses are due to our injustice towards them.

All the sicknesses attacking people are due to former or current crimes. Nothings remains unpunished! The germs, now poisoning the human body, are nothing but the poison of fear and hatred, which the cattle, chickens, lambs felt towards the man who killed and butchered them. Is that possible? It is possible. The same way an offensive word can poison and destroy human body, the fear and hatred of animals, which man butchers, poison his body.

Certain sicknesses, bad thoughts and desires, which occur in you, are caused by certain mammals. In order to be relieved of all these suffering, you must mellow down you attitudes towards animals. Often a dog's hatred may have the same effect as the hatred of a man. Don't think that animals' thoughts are very weak. No they are very dangerous for the world.

The culture itself carries poisons in itself. They way people are doing, if they don't correct themselves, they will always carry with themselves their misery. How are miseries born? At first miseries are born of the unnatural selection of food. In America there are statistics, showing that about 35-40 million pigs are killed every year. Millions of animals are killed in Europe as well, as nobody takes into consideration their feelings. The Scripture says: "Whoever slaughters an ox, is as if he is slaughtering a man". This shows that God is not content with the death of the animals. And here's what I'm asking: how would human culture be improved, when a large number of mammals are being killed every year? These mammals, when being killed, they created the most unfavourable conditions for the human culture, and those religious people, Christians, they open the Bible every day and read that the Lord has created all that for people. Time created them. After that plants came, which redeem animals' lives. Animals, on their part, redeem people's live. And then people say that it is allowed to eat the animals for the good of mankind. This is an internal permission. This is one of the most unnatural types of food. Man may dare to do a lot of unnatural things!

When I am talking to you in this way, I don't want to make you vegetarians in this way. This is unnatural. Now I want you all to have a desire for all those principles, it takes to built a man. If you want to have an excellent mind, an excellent stomach and excellent lungs, you must pick the necessary food.

The main task of the animals is to collect magnetism. While animals are healthy, people will be healthy as well, and as soon animals start being sick, people will also be sick. That is why we must be friendly to animals, in order to be able to make use of the magnetic powers which they store in themselves.

Due to the cutting down of forests and the killing of mammals, people are subjected to great sufferings, without being able to help themselves. They don't even suspect that animals and plants are reservoirs of vital powers for the growth and development of man. By exterminating mammals, their vital powers are dispersed in space. As long as people are unable to connect directly to the powers of nature, they are deprived of those very powers, which they would receive from animals.

The immense extermination of mammals creates abnormalities in nature. Most diseases are due to the killing of mammals and birds. As far as that extermination does not stop their evolution, al the powers, which are to form their wellbeing, remain unused and thus chaos comes upon the world, which is the reason for the various diseases. Do you know what happens after the arbitrary spillage of this animal blood? Its vapours produce various serums and cultures for the harmful germs, which produce all the evils in the organic world. In order to achieve balance in nature, it had to shed about one million kilos of blood, to balance those animals' blood. But now, this war lead to the shedding of about 2 million kilos of blood.

In order to achieve a balance in nature, about 100 million kilos of blood are to be shed, to balance animals' blood – and this is what wars do.

They way water is needed to wash the clothes, to water the flowers, the same way – if we sometimes commit minor crimes, blood will be needed for cleaning. As long as crimes are big, millions of people will have to die, in order to cleanse the soaked earth of the crimes, so that we can live.

You will shed a lot of blood, before you are cleansed.

Your happiness in the world lies on the sufferings of those tiny creatures, which serve you. You, who consider yourselves very noble, go and ask the small creatures what do they think of your nobility. All the sheep, oxen, lambs, chickens, ducks, all those birds have an attitude towards you, all of them have a special opinion of men. All the smaller creatures shout in one voice, that man is an extremely cruel being. If you ask the trees, they will also say as well: "Man is horrible, merciless!" and then you would ask: "Why the Lord has created the world this way?" No! The lord created the world to be good, but we and all those people before us, have spoiled it. The way the external world is spoiled, it affects our inner selves. The world is made in such a way that when the master suffers, the servants suffer as well, and vice-versa.

The same goods God has provided man with, these have also been provided to the trees, and flowers, and little flies and fish, and birds and all the mammals.

One day the chicken complained about her master, saying that he always took her eggs away and ate them. At the same time the sheep complained about her master, that he sheared its wool and milked it. The master rejected chickens complaints, in this way: "The chicken should be thankful that I don't take its life. And as for its eggs, I just relieve it. It lays about 150 eggs every ear, and it can hatch not more than 25-30 of them. What is it going to do with the other eggs?" and this is how he replied to sheep's complaints: "You have a lamb, which you feed on your milk. Now I just take a part of your milk. If I don't shear your wool, you will suffer – heat will torment you." And the cow complained about her master but he told it as well that it had no right to complain – it have more milk than its calf needed. And the calf eats milk no more than a year, and after that the milk is free. And therefore I have the right to take it.

Man is in harmony with nature, as well as with the Divine world, while it makes use of the surplus of goods. If he wants to use all the goods, he disturbs that harmony. Nature preserves a part of the goods for itself, something like an emergency stock. Whoever dares to lay hands on that stock, he breaches the great rules of life.

There is a human habit, which people themselves have introduced in their lives, and which they must eliminate themselves. In order to escape these rules, people have to eliminate the human rules and impose God's, the Divine nature of man. Every person can find the divine understanding in himself – nowhere else. No matter how hungry a person may be, he will never cut a piece of meat from his leg or from another place. One would never let himself eat from his own meat. If he cuts off a portion of his own meat and tries to eat it – he will feel utmost repulsion. If you feel such a repulsion when it comes to you, why don't you feel the same about others? Why a hungry person, when there is nobody around, can starve to death, without being tempted to eat from his own body? Why he can starve to death also when there are other people around? In both cases a person should not touch the meat of his neighbour, of himself, or of an animal. This is God's understanding. If we apply that in life, there will be no death.

Now we have abandoned that true life and take away a life, which is not God's will: we take an animal, without it being willing, and take away its life. We don't ask it for its consent. It wants to live, but we eat it. This is not a way to live. The great misfortunes, the great sicknesses, neurasthenia--, the consumption, which come to this world, are partly due to the extermination of mammals and the cutting down of forests. All the sicknesses are due to the unnatural situation, which we allow in the world. We allow ourselves what we should not allow, because we don't have a sacred feeling. We allow ourselves to cut a tree, a plant – just like that – out of mere fancy. There are plants that have lived for 100, 150, 200 years and in America there are animals, which have lived 1 500-2 000 years. And Americans cut them down. But because of this arbitrary clearing of forests, of the arbitrary extermination of mammals, there is no other country in the world with so much neurasthenia and so many nervous diseases, as America, and there are no people with so damaged teeth as Americans. You may say that this is a mere coincidence. The law is the same everywhere. We cannot do whatever we want! We must do what conforms to the laws of the living nature.

The true man eats through his mind.

Man is situated amidst two systems — the mental and sympathetic nervous system. and after he departs from this world, these two systems continue to function in the other world.

You may say: "After death the body melts away, it rots and disappears". No there is something which does not disappear from the body even after man's death. On the contrary after one dies, that is precisely when he feels even more that is connected to thousands and millions more creatures. So – no matter what people you used to be connected with before your death, you will feel this connection the strongest. If you were connected to people of the stomach, for example, that connection you will feel most. If you used to be connected with people of the lungs – the strongest connection you will feel, will be that with them. Therefore don't think that when you go to the other world, you will be free. If on the Earth you used to be connected to people living only for their stomachs, in the other world, you will be connected with their desires, which will constantly bother you.

When somebody dies, if he used to love indulging himself in eating, when the physical body disappears, the capability of eating and drinking disappears as well, however the desire persists, and that is why that person continues to go about those people who eat and drink – he urges them, but remains hungry, for he has no physical organs.

You will find people, who are like you. The kind of person one is, it is that kind of people he will find: whoever likes to gossip, he will find people like him – gossipers; whoever loves money, he will find others who love money as well; whoever likes to drink – he will find drinkers like him. All day they will walk about in the world, and when they find somebody drinking, they will say: "Leave something for me". The one who likes smoking tobacco will find those who like smoking too. The ladies, who like to put make up on their faces, will find others alike. Do you know how funny souls are? A soul thinks that it has hair, it has a face, that it sits in front of the mirror, putting makeup on it. There is no makeup! Then it puts on a dress and other clothing, but there is none. Things are much different there. It takes years, until a soul acknowledges that it is just a dream. It is just like, when you are dreaming that someone is chasing you, or when you are dreaming that you are rich.

There is a whole lot of them around a gluttonous person; they see you, stay by your side and start giving you advice. But they only love the smell: when you are cooking fish, when they smell it – they feel great pleasure.

I've heard people say: "Couldn't God make people so that they didn't have to eat?" Of course he could. After you die, you will no longer eat. After you die, you will go to people and watch them eat, and you will want to eat as well, but won't be able to do it. You will look at all the tables, and see everybody eating, but you wouldn't be able to even taste a dis. You will only live with your past experiences. You will try to lift a fork, and fail. It takes several thousand souls to lift a spoon and put it in the mouth. And three or four weeks will pass until they lift it, and food will be spoiled. They can't lift a human spoon, because if they try to do so, they will entangle themselves in the karmic law of cause and effect. Some people wonder how a spirit is unable to lift a spoon. How can you do that – there is vortex – if you try to jump over it, you will fall in the abyss – nothing will remain of you – this is a vortex, you can't jump over. So some people do not understand this law. Not just one soul – even if thousands gather together, they will still be unable to lift a spoon. And a single person can lift not one, but as many spoons he wants.

Speaking of existence and non-existence, this does not mean that existence is something real, and non-existence – something unreal. Non-existence is a place of suffering, of hell. The position of a person, going into non-existence is terrible. He has the desire to see, but everything around him is darkness; he wants to eat – he is extremely hungry, but there's nothing to eat; he is thirsty – he wants to drink water, but he can't satisfy his thirst. From the perspective of the existence, of material life, non-existence is a life of imagination. Why? Because things there are not fulfilled. The non-existence is a life of thirst and hunger, an eternal striving to satisfy something, which is impossible to satisfy under those conditions. That is why, while man is on the Earth, and still in existence, he must study the laws of good, so that he can satisfy his hunger and thirst. It is only good, as a great rational principle that can relieve a man of his thirst and hunger. Good is the foundation of the great law of liberation. To be good, this means to be liberated from slavery, i.e. from the world of limitations and death. By "death we mean those conditions, which deprive a man of all the goods of life. This is the reason why people fear death. Those, who don't understand death think that it will liberate them from the hardships of life. But it shall not liberate them, but take them to non-existence. The thought of the non-existence is an acid, which frets and destroys. If a person thinks too long about non-existence, at the end he will evaporate. Many philosophers evaporated, for the mere reason that they fell in the area of non-existence. No ordinary person, mortal has ever solved or will ever be able to solve the issue of non-existence. Whoever dealt with that matter, achieved nothing,...

"Then why was I ever born?" To be good. "How can I become good?" By satisfying your thirst and hunger with goodness. This is a rational nutrition. This is how you can understand Christ's words that man can live not only on bread, but also on any rational Word, coming from God. Whoever eats goodness, he never dies, he becomes the master of the conditions and enters the area of existence. So only good is real. Only that, which does not change or perish or can ever be destroyed is real. Because good never changes, it is never lost and it does not disappear, it is real. Is water real? For us it is not real, because it changes. For other beings, however, water is real. Hard matter is real for us.

And now many of you are in non-existence, you say: "I can't do that ". So you are in non-existence. And when you manage to do whatever you are doing, you are in existence. If you can't create something, you are once again in non-existence, and we strive to get into the existence of life. I speak of the existence in a positive sense. Not that non-existence is not a reality, but non-existence are the most horrible things, one can imaging. Some say: "May this never happen!"

Imagine that you are in non-existence, you have all the desires, thirst, hunger and striving and you preserve them, not having any conditions for what is inside of you. Do you know what suffering that will be! Not to occupy any space and to think that you have something. To want to eat, to feel that, to suffer and have nothing to eat. You see nothing around you, everything is emptiness, there is no space, you are in the dark. In what position will you be? It is non-existence. From the perspective of our current lives, everything is imagination, a hallucination. It is a hallucination, because you have nothing to realize in the non-existence. It is true that you can't eat, because you have nothing, nothing exists, but at the same time, in you there is an impulse, which is called thirst and hunger.

You want to eat, but you have no stomach, to put the food into. You want to catch somebody, but you have no hands, you want to go somewhere, but you have no feet. Here's what I ask: if you find yourselves in that world and you say that you have no hands, feet, eyes, you still have the desire, the desire of life is in you, and you have no life to satisfy your desire, do you know what you condition will be? Years ago, an American wrote a book — "Letters from the other world", telling about the punishment of the rich. He said that the rich people, who have not done any good in this world, in the other world these people will sit in front of abundant tables with plenty of the best dishes, but once they try to get to the food, the tables go away. They walk after them, approach them, but the tables get away once again and so they constantly go around the food, but can't get.

Probably 10-15 years ago in America they published a letter from the other world. A man wrote to his father. We have everything, he said, but we can't eat it. You have everything you can think of. He said that the tables were full of all dishes one can imagine. "There is everything on it, whatever you we may want. But if we try to approach the table - it moves away. Whatever we try to approach, it moves away." Do you think everything in this world is eatable? You go along a road, the food is there on display, but you haven't got a single dime in your pocket. You can look it, but can't eat it. In that world you can't eat if you don't have money. There you need money as well. In that world you can't take anything from a cook, if you haven't loved him – he will give you nothing. If you love him, the table is not moving. If you don't love him, the table moves, runs away from you. Isn't it so in this world as well? A girl, who doesn't love a boy, runs away from him. And if she loves him, she speaks with him. If boy loves a girl, he stays as well. If he doesn't love her, he runs. The law is the same.

When do you rejoice today? When you roast a pig, a chicken, a turkey, when you pour yourselves some wine, then you sit at the table, start rattling the forks, clinking glasses, drinking for health, for wellbeing throughout the world. However these chickens and lambs are not pleased with your joy, they don't share it. Your joy is their sorrow. One day the relations will change: your fats will nourish the grass, which the sheep will peacefully graze. This will be the retribution for their meat, which you used for years. This the great karmic law. Christ says: "When we so understand life, all the miseries will disappear and light will be bright". You don't know why sheep graze the grass. This is a temporary method, for in the future food will be consumed through the entire body, through its pores, without chewing. You may ask: "What should we do?" You must always keep open, light and clear the eye, God has put into your souls, so that you can bath in His light and warmth.

Often people laugh at the Egyptians, who worshiped Apis. It is this Apis, who mellowed the temper of the Egyptians, who were very realistic people. You may say that this is a delusion. No, they believed that a deity lived in Apis, and they worshiped that deity. Egyptians spiritualized animals and said that there was something Divine in them. They believed that a deity is embodied in every animal, and thus they respected and worshiped all the animals. This is how they viewed Apis, the cat – as a holy animal. Nobody could kill an animal there. They were greatly honoured.

In Isaiah, Chapter 77, it is said that when somebody killed an ox it was the same as killing a man. The prophet Isaiah, who lived more than 3 000 years ago, he had higher morals than people nowadays. After all that people say: "Christ Resurrected!" Christ resurrected, but not for your oxen, sheep, chickens. Until Christ is resurrected for all the living creatures, for your oxen, sheep and lambs, you won't be allowed to the Kingdom of the Lord. I use words "ox", "chicken", „sheep" figuratively. 2 000 years ago Christ said: "You shall love your neighbour as yourself". There is something missing in this line, it is not whole. That is why I add: "You shall love all living creatures, from the smallest to the biggest, as yourself ".

"DO YOU LOVE ME?"

Non-eating is a crime. But is there such a law in the world? The sheep that grazes in the field, is right. The wolf, when he eats the sheep is wrong, he is considered guilty. The sheep, eating grass, is not considered guilty. And the wolf, after he eats a sheep is considered guilty. What are the motives for declaring the wolf guilty? The wolf is guilty of eating sheep's food. Because, while it collected food — sheep can be considered ruminant animals – so after it collects food, to process it, the wolf stole that from it. This is his fault. He has violated sheep's rights. I.e. in nature no creature is allowed to take away another creature's food. If it takes another creature's food, it has already violated the law. That wolf forms a static situation.

The wolf – these are the hardships in the world. In fact the wolf can't eat the sheep, because there is a law in nature, stating that what is eaten, actually breeds more. If wolves had stopped eating sheep, sheep would have decreased in numbers. So, until there are hardships and suffering in the world, the knowledge in the world will increase.

Happiness, in the full sense of this word, is preconditioned by the good disposition of all rational beings. In order to be happy, you have to be rational. You must live among rational creatures, so that their collective disposition you can feel as happiness. This means that you have to be connected to the rationality, with Divine Love. When people are unable to find happiness, this means that they want to keep happiness only to themselves. There is no such happiness in the world. Such happiness is bought by the Bulgarian with money. He buys a pig and feeds it all the winter and throughout the summer – three-four times a day he brings it food, gives it water, scratches its back. The pig makes a sound of pleasure, thus wanting to say: "See how happy I am! I finally found a master, who takes care of me." Everything is fine. But then Christmas comes, there is squeaking, grilling. Now the Bulgarian wants to know if the swine was happy. He eats the swine in order to be happy.

When you eat a pig it becomes your tenant. If you eat a chicken – it again becomes your tenant.

If you eat pork, pig's cells will be engrafted in you. If you eat only meat food, the accumulation of these cells will bring upon you the character of the animals you have eaten. Pig's cells are unnatural, they require a lot of energy, so that a man can keep them working – they are both very lazy and very destructive.

Why is pork unhygienic? When you eat pork, pig's cells will become a part of you. Pig's nature will become a part of you. Pig's cells are very lazy – it takes more energy to make them work, than they can produce for you.

You often fail to notice that the shapes, existing in nature express conditions. You want to have a large body. Nature made attempts. Let's say that you have the shape of man and the shape of a bee. A man says that he eats too little. The food of how many bees, can a man, who eats a little devour in one sitting? With one of your lunches, 30 thousand bees can live for a week. You think that our life, which we have. Is very economic! You are not at economic for the nature. You eat three times a day – so much, and still you think that you eat very little. We eat so much, because we have very little income. Of all the food that you take – very little is assimilated in your body.

Good food is that, which can organize the powers of a human body. Each cell must be organized, living, to take active participation in the functioning of the human organs, if it does not take such participation, it is a dead, harmful cell.

Where does the word "swine" come from? I speak of the swine, as a symbol of the creature, which values life. It loves life so much that when it feels it is about to be butchered, it starts squeaking so loud that people gather around it. It has a strong desire to live.

The grass, fruits, which you eat, they rejoice, while the animal, when being butchered to be eaten, is not content and this discontent will get into you.

The cells, which come in us from the animal kingdom, they spend more and produce less, and the plant cells, which get into us, spend less and produce more. Apart from that, the animal cells, which we take in use, are too disobedient.

A meal, which pleases someone, is unpleasant to another. Why is that? How can you explain this? It's a matter of taste. However there are other, more significant reasons. The pleasant food is that, which brings you what you want. Unpleasant is that food, which takes more and gives less. When such food takes from you and gets outside, you feel poorer.

Why is pork unhygienic? Pig's cells have a great individuality. When they enter the body, you must put another 20 cells in to protect a single cell. They get out in the first convenient moment. Such a person will consume the food for 100 men, and do the work of 5 men. Why is he like that – don't judge him for his outside. All those, who eat pork – they all pay. And here's what I say: we don't need great individuals, we need cells, which are in harmony with us. That food, in nature – when a living creature takes it in, it must remain in harmony with its life.

When the cells of the meat food enter the body, it must use ten times more energy to keep them in, i.e. to place them in their relevant places and put them to work. And how much can these cells work? Does a man need such workers, who bring one thing, but take away another? Pork is delicious, but it brings one thing and takes away ten things. You will only eat food, which brings ten things, and takes away one. This is the fruit food. This unnatural state, in which we find ourselves, along with the entire cultural world, is due to the meat food.

The power we receive from eating fruits and vegetables, is much more lasting than the power, we get from meet. More power is used to assimilate meat food, and then what is the use?

Because the vibrations of the mammals are lower than those of man, he trips, when he eats them and can't develop. The meat food is full of vibrations of the animal passions, and in this respect the plant food is pure. Man must eat pure food, so that his cells obey him. If a person eats pork for too long, he will obtain a pig's character, and if he eats chicken – he will obtain chicken's character.

Bulgarians eat more bread, to become softer. Some other peoples eat a lot of meat — at breakfast, at lunch and at dinner — and acquire a rough activeness in a lower area. A lot of time will pass until a people learn not to use meat food.

If you eat pork, you will have the concepts of a swine: you will dig the ground and think that you have dug yourself the pears, falling from the tree. In one respect the swine is right — by digging the earth it digs out the Jerusalem artichoke. And if something falls from above – it believes it comes from below. It searches for everything below.

It is not bad to eat a chicken or a hen. But that chicken will get into you and start digging. The one eating too many chickens cannot keep to the truth. Those who eat too many hens – there are such old grannies, they are gossipers – going around spreading news. Such a granny comes to your house, saying: "Hear something new: our priest went on pilgrimage. Don't tell anybody!" Then she goes to another place and says: "Our priest went on pilgrimage. Don't tell anybody!" And so before night the entire village knows that the priest is on pilgrimage.

If you eat rabbit, you won't become a proper man. If you want to become a man, don't ever eat rabbit.

After the wolf takes sheep's life, and its capability of developing, where does it go? It is eaten by the wolf. Now is that sheep still existing? If you make a mixture of iron and pure gold in equal proportions – for example – half a kilo of iron and hold, do you think that the golden particles will become iron? As much as you may mix that the iron cannot eat the gold. Where is the gold? Do you think a wolf can eat a sheep? It just deceives itself – the sheep remains a sheep. These are philosophical questions. You say: "We know that the wolf ate the sheep". The wolf only destroys the shape, deprives the sheep of its shape, but it cannot transform the sheep life and make it its own – a wolf's life. After eating the sheep, the wolf becomes meek and calm as a sheep. It says to itself: "Why did I eat the sheep?" But then, when he gets hungry — the sheep has already released itself from him, it has gone, he once again starts circling the flock. And because, it started loving the firs one, it continues to look for it. It says: "I was restless, used to have a bad disposition, and when I ate the sheep, I calmed down. I will find another sheep to achieve that again."

Wolf's crime is not in his eating the sheep, but in destroying something, he has not created. Therefore in the world we are not allowed to destroy what we have not created. We can only change what we have created. Or to say that differently: we are not allowed to destroy something created by God.

Sometimes we say: "Let's be honest!" A pig is given water and food 4-5 times a day 4-5, they prepare it for Christmas and when that day comes, on the date of Christ's birth, all the pigs start crying. Then Bulgarians stab the pigs in their hearts, or cut their throats. A sometimes see a brother, a bit drunk, then Christmas comes – you look at him – he fell ill. And sometimes such brother may get stabbed killed – someone attacked and stabbed him, and that brother is gone. And you say: "He was healthy ". Wasn't he taken out of the pigsty? Where did they put? We now deceive ourselves, saying that he went to the Lord. You are right. Pigs, when they are out of their pigsties, where do they go? The pig, while in the pigsty, was in a muddy house. When it goes out of the mud, it goes to the people, and is now respected and honoured, so it sits at the table of the humans. The pig goes to live in humans.

Everything that happens in life is good-. Because we consider things from a relative position – it is not good for me, but it's good for the whole. It is not good to eat a hen – yes – it is not good for it, but it's good for you. The hen is now put to a place, where it can no longer commit crimes – that hen is in a better place – instead of suffering in the world, it will come and live in you. The hen has lost nothing – it only wins — it now sits as a true son or a son-in-law.

From God's perspective, it is not sinful to eat a hen. If a river flows into another river – is there a crime? If the smaller river flows into the bigger one, if then rivers merge and form a big river, what crime can there be? If a man has eaten ten hens, the lives of those hens just flowed into his own life – what crime can this be? The living person thinks much better than a hen, which just goes around and digs. What is better: to think well or to dig well? The worst of all is that when you eat the hen, instead of it thinking like you, you start digging like the hen. All the evil is in that, after eating the hen, people don't think better, but dig better – this is the bad thing. As soon as the hen starts digging inside of you, you are now in a lower life. Therefore, if the hen in you starts digging, you have become bad. If the hen in you starts thinking, you have become good. I praise the hen, when it suffers. And I pity the man, when he rejoices. If you are happy, for eating the hen, so that you can dig, I pity you. If you suffer that you must teach the hen to think like you, if you suffer in this way, I am happy for you. And I say: you are a clever man.

The wolf may eat a sheep, if he wants to become meeker, but he will surely become meek, because now the wolf is much meeker than he used to be. And people, who eat sheep and hens, will tell you that they eat sheep, because they want to be pretty, they you hens, for they want to have wings, like angels. And you have the right to eat them.

I can say nothing bad of this frog – it has to eat flies. And why does it eat flies? I will tell you that. Because the fly, being a flying creature, lives in a higher position, and the frog, which also strives at flying in the air, it wants to assume the vibrations of the fly, to develop them and to fly. Why does the wolf eat sheep? It must eat sheep to become meek, because when we eat good things, we become good.

Some birds love fish. They go above the sea and start telling the fishes: "Come out of the water, and see that there is another world around you!" If they obey and come out of the water, the birds immediately snatch and eat them. "What is that, didn't you say you loved us?" "Yes, I loved you, nut I ate you so that you know me." Now, let me explain why do birds eat fish. In order to understand that, I must first explain why people like eating hens. After a man preaches to a hen to believe in something, he finally butchers it. The hen speaks from inside of them men: "It is still too early for me, to study this doctrine, you should have waited a little." Is it precisely like that, it is not known, but the explanation is about correct. If, after the fish enters the man, and loses its conscience of a fish, and believes what you have preached, it shall have the consciousness to sacrifice itself, but if, after it enters the man, it only thinks of water, then it has not elevated yet. It says: "It is very nice here, but I'd rather be back in the water".

God is a consciousness, where all the other consciousnesses live. And he tries to adjust all these consciousnesses in Himself. God wants to tell us: "When you need food, turn to Me, I will satisfy you, do not turn to each other for food ". If, however, you need food, instead of turning to God for that and addressing Him, you go for food to the henhouse. The hen cackles, cackles, but you wouldn't listen, just saying: "It was written there, that the hen was created for men". If God lives in a hen, you have the right to eat it. But there are hens, in which God does not live. Therefore you can't eat such hens. God lives in some animals, and in others – does not. Currently the Lord lives more in fruits. The outside of the fruit is just a garment, you can eat that. Te fruit says: "When you eat me, plant my seed somewhere, so that the complete balance can be restored ".

According to God's law, the hungry can eat everywhere. But there are some limitations: he can't pick an apple from the garden, if there is no water nearby so that he can wash it. He can't eat it, without turning his eyes to thank the Lord for sending down light to make that apple. So that it is known that he ate it. Always, when you have not prayed and have eaten a fruit, you have committed a crime. It is a crime to eat without permission.

You must understand the living laws. The entire wealth – the coal, mines – all that belongs to a certain society. Why do all these sufferings come upon men? These are interests that we pay. You catch a hen, and butcher it. You say: "The Lord has made the world this way". And then you suffer. You speculate wrongly. This hen belongs to a society. You must ask the Lord if you can butcher it. You have a sheep and you shear it. It belongs to another world, and you must ask are you entitled to take something from it. And not to act, the way you are not allowed to.

"Do not kill!" Do not butcher hens, don't eat them. According to the new testament, when you take an apple, you shall come to love it and say to it: "Would you like to visit come to me?" If it wouldn't – don't take it and don't eat it. If you understand the law. If you hear the words: "I will sacrifice myself for you", let it come, that apple shall loose nothing. When it enters you, you will plant it in your garden. You will plant each seed of that apple in your Garden of Eden and it will be a golden tree in your thought. If all the apples you have eaten, become golden trees in you, this eating shall be proper. This must be the idea of the new.

If you come to slaughter an animal – do it with Love. It must feel content that you will butcher it, it should lay down its own head alone - then you may butcher it.

Some rely on the words of Christ: "If you don't eat My flesh and don't drink My blood, you have no life". You take that literally. You can eat a hen. You will ask it: "Do you love me, are you ready to sacrifice yourself for me?" If it is ready, if it loves you, you can eat it. If you take it out of the hennery, without asking it, this is a human deed.

When you have nothing to eat and you want to butcher a hen, you must first ask it: "What do you want – do you want us both to die, or do you want me to live, and you to die, so that you come and live in me?" Now I'm presenting to you an idea, in which I want you to believe, but first you must try it. When you try it, then you will remember my words. What you have not tried is not true. The things that have been tried, on the other hand, are facts. The hen or lamb, which you have eaten, one day they will become your sons or daughters — nothing more. You say that you have eaten a hen. I am glad that you have eaten it, for one day the hen will become your daughter, and the lamb – your son. In this way they come out of the position, in which they are today and will transcend to a higher condition. This is the meaning of the words that Christ said: "If you don't eat My flesh and don't drink My blood, you have no life in you". Because when a man eats a lamb, then lamb's soul merges with the soul of that man and in the future that lamb will have better opportunities for its ascend.

There is no wolf, which – having eaten 10 million sheep – has remained a wolf. When it eats the last of the 10 million sheep, then his evolution starts, he starts experiencing the background of the sheep. And here's what I say: if you are a wolf and eat 10 million sheep, then you will become a sheep. Then the reverse process will start — the experiencing of sheep's history. Don't understand that literally, take it in its broad sense, only as clarification. When told like this, it is only a clarification.

Life has several phrases. When the seed falls on the ground, it is the first phrase, the first step; this is where the great suffering starts. That seed will undergo a crisis. After that the second process starts — the sprouting. This is just the path, through which life manifests itself. After the initial growing – it will flower. The flowering is the third phase. The fourth phase is the fertilization. There is another phase. And finally comes the ripening of the fruit – this is the sixth phase. The fruit must be tried by someone. And spiritually, when someone dies on the Earth, this is similar to the fruit, as long as the fruit has not fallen off. When somebody dies on Earth, he will be met by God, as we meet the ripe fruits, collected in a basket, we take them with the same love. This is the comparison. The one, living on the earth, will say: "What's the use of eating a fruit?" Fruit's life transcends to a higher sphere. Something remains of the fruit. It is precisely man, who gives. Man is the best condition for the fruit tree to grow. After you've eaten a fruit, that fruit grows in you. If you have eaten it out of Love, it is not lost, it grows.

Eating is a law of familiarization. You can't get familiar with a fruit, if you don't eat it. Therefore, when you eat the fruit, you will find out if it loves you or not. If it causes you stomach-ache, that fruit does not love you; if it brings you joy in the stomach, then this fruit loves you, you will get to know him. If it loves you, it will open place, it will enter the brain, you will walk it around that great world. The fruit will start learning within you.

This process is a conversation. Eating is nothing but a conversation with that apple. "Shall I take you to the reception room!" You converse with it. Then you will speak with the apple in the lungs, and at last you will climb up in the sanctuary, in the church, and there you will converse with the apple. After you take the apple up to the brain, what will you do? You will create a new shape for the apple, you will pay its ticket to get back where it came from. You, like a poet, will write an entire poem for the apple. You will say: "Goodbye and farewell!" And the apple is gone. And the apple is content, because it is happy to ascend, and you are content as well.

Here's what I say: You must form in yourselves a right thought. A right thought produces three processes: the mechanic, organic and mental processes. When you go through these three processes, you will create something in yourselves. A good thought is always created, when these three processes or the three worlds are connected like the wheel that moves. All the misfortunes in life result from our suspension of the processes-. As soon as we suspend the processes-, life becomes monotonous and then nothing is achieved.

`Each apple, you start eating, is a kiss. You not only kiss it, but eat it. When sometimes you kiss, you say: "I feel like eating you!" Everybody, who kisses you now, even your beloved ones, when they kiss you on Earth, they say: "Once I ate you like an apple, and now I have a law inside – it is not allowed to eat people, I will just kiss you ". Each kiss is a reflection of a complete devouring. When you kiss a man, you must understand the meaning: once upon a time, handsome guys like you used to be eaten, roasted. Now he is not roasted, but kissed. The kiss shows that a man has progressed from that condition of the past. The kiss has come in a new form. Or to say that more clearly: if a person has changed his life and his deeds, then God has already infused some reason in him. Because until that reason, that Divine portion, gets inside you, it is very hard for you to even reconcile with life itself.

There was a time when people didn't even know what Love is. The wolf, when it gets to love a sheep – it eats it. The child, when it gets to love an apple – eats it. The spider, when it gets to love a fly – eats it. The first rule of Love: when somebody gets to love you, he eats you. The strong always eats the week. He eats the week alone, and the week collectively eat the strong.

All good things are eaten, and all bad things – are not to be eaten. You eat a hen, because you love it, nothing more. Because eating meat is love. What of you eating your beloved one? And all people can't live together, for they love each other. As soon as they start loving each other, people can no longer live together for they love each other. When people get to love each other, they can no longer live well. Because everybody in his love, wants to eat the other. When Christ came on Earth, he knew that and said: "If you don't eat My flesh and don't drink My blood, you have no life in you". He did not say: "Whoever eats my head, he shall not see another bright day", but he said: "Whoever does not eat me, he shall not have eternal life. And I pity him, who does not eat me!" This is what I can say about human consciousness.

We, the people of the physical world, are the stomach of Existence, of Cosmos. Danger, sin is in us. Why do all people only think of eating and drinking. They understand life very shallowly. All scholars, whatever they are, think first of eating. When the writer writes, he thinks mostly of writing something good, so that it is sold better. A preacher thinks and preaches well, in order to be liked, so that more people come to hear his preaching. If you observe people, you will see that everybody has in himself a concealed covetousness. They speak of god, but something else hides behind that idea of God. We don't want it, don't realize it, but there is such a thing. You want to talk nicely, you want to draw well, you want to play well – you want to be liked in everything. You want to be liked in playing as well. Everything is made so that there is nothing spiritual in them. Money or some sort of interest is the reason for everything done here. And even the reason for every perfect deed is something human. Why? Because we enter the stomach of Existence.

Now, the way people believe, all that has a mercenary goal. It is not selfless. If I eat a hen out of love, it is love not of the hen, but of myself. I come first and the hen comes next. And in real Love, things are not like that. This is how you can cope sometimes. I go to the hen, and it tells me: "Don't eat me! I will soon lay an egg, eat the egg, instead of me." And then I give in and eat the egg, instead of the hen. You go to a fruit tree, and when you stretch out to cut the tree, it says: "Don't cut me down, I will give you a lot of fruit during this year – you can eat that ". Leave that tree alone, don't cut it!

I encounter a hen and tell it: "I love you very much". And that I, for I love it, will eat it. It says: "I don't want you to love me this way". Now you think that it is God's will that I eat the hen. I don't know, it is said: may animals be conquered! But I don't know if you may eat the hen. Only one person has ever said that he has to be eaten, but it was Christ. And he is the most judicious. He says: "If you don't eat my flesh, and you don't drink my blood …". Which hen has ever said: "If you don't eat me, you have no life in yourselves"?

At first animals searched for food through touch, it is the simplest method. But they found it to be very impractical so they replaced it. After that they started finding their food through tasting, smelling, listening, and finally they came to looking. The most practical method is looking. Therefore, when you want to look, you mean something close to your heart, or close to your mind. Take the primary profound reason, underlying in consciousness.

The first question is: to love, or to be loved. And they you can decide when the desire "to love" has occurred in consciousness. And when the desire "to be loved" has occurred in the consciousness. Just make a simple experiment, it goes, as follows: take a good cherry. Do the experiment, when you are not hungry. At first you want to hold it, you love it, but the hungrier you get, the more its beauty disappears in your consciousness, to be replaced by the desire to it that cherry. Note the main changes, occurring in your consciousness. There are a lot of cherries – do this experiment. Take one or five good cherries, but you must be full – let them stay. See how the desire to eat them will slowly come upon you. So you have reached in your consciousness the desire to be loved. So you will say to the cherry: "Until now I loved you, and now you will love me". The one who loves, will be devoured. The smaller eat the bigger. It is always like that in the world. It is not the big that is strong, but the small.

The question is how should we love. Christ has answered that question in a different way. Until then, everybody who loved, ate those who were loved by them. This was what the old love was. And Christ, when he came on Earth, in the new Love, he said: O love the others, not to eat them, but I, loving them, want them to eat Me. So the opposite thing happens. Therefore, if you love the others and want to eat them – this is the old love, where all the crimes happen. The new Love is in this: when you love somebody, he should eat you. And all the goodness comes from that eating. And everything is built upon that. If you are not eaten, you are not in the new Love, and when you are eaten, goodness is born then. When people eat you, then you will built goodness. After people eat Christ, he shall enter them and teach them how to love. If you eat them, they will teach you whatever they know. If you eat a hen, it will teach you to dig, if you eat a pig, it will also teach you to dig. The pig with its muzzle, has surrendered to digging the earth. So all of you deal with digging everywhere. Because the swine digs with its nose – its muzzle, and the muzzle is an expression of the human intelligence, of the human thought.

Now we have nothing to fight against that. You loose heart, but you also have the role of the flour in the bag. You say: "What will become of me – I am flour ". A master will come, then he will take this flour, put it in the hutch, he will warm-up some water, put the flour in the water, then knead these parts and make a bread, then he will bake the best loaf there is.

From the flour that you are now, the Lord will make the best bread. He won't even ask you whether you want it or not.

You say: "I am free". Freedom is something relative. One day the Lord will come, he will untie the bag, bring some water and knead the flour, then put it in the oven. Then those, who know how to eat will come, and you will have the experience of the apple, of the plum and the pear. Those creatures, which will eat you, will be angels, they will chew you a bit in angels' mouths. You'll be blessed if all of you can become such a bread for eating! My respect and honour to all those of you, who will become such fresh breads. Have faith in the One, with whose providence now we live, Him, who made the Sun shine, in order to help you, Him, who made the stars and the entire nature. His providence is good upon us.

WINE

The devil also has a kitchen. The Lord made water, and the devil made wine. The Lord made water, and the devil made spirits, the absinthes and cognacs. There are many creations of the devil. Now I am speaking of the devil honestly, as a scholar. The devil says: "It's not the Lord, who can make things. He only created water, and I can make a number of spirits. In this respect I am a better master than the Lord. The water, which the Lord has made, only serves to cool down people, and the beverages I make can also be used for entertainment. When they drink of my drinks, people will acquire inspiration. The Lord is not the only one who can make many things – I can too. Therefore put your faith in me."

Modern science and life interest me, and with all the contradictions I encounter, I still manage to find many useful things. I admire much more a barefooted child than a rich and well-dress one. The poor child is excellent, because you can talk to it, it is humble. The well-dressed child has some external forms, dishonest, through which it wants to show that it is not simple. I encounter a very drunk person. He apologizes and says: "I am sorry, sir, I am a jackass, I am very drunk". Here's what I say to him: "You are not a jackass, because the jackass does not drink, but you are an honest man, for which I respect you". Sometimes a person, when he gets drunk, he can become a bourgeois, because a working man never gets drunk. All the drunkards are bourgeois.

More than 15 years ago I was in the Novi Pazar area, and there was an evangelist there, a Greek – he used to read the Gospel all they long and interpret it, and he was the owner of the pub in the village, and sold brandy, but he was so scrupulous that, when somebody came, he said: "Listen, I don't want you to get drunk, you should drink just a little". They asked him: "Then why do you sell us brandy?" "This is the only way I can find you ", was his reply.

Those, who eat meat, smoke and drink, cannot rejuvenate.

The occult student is not allowed to drink alcohol, beer, boza (millet-ale), lemonades. In very rare cases, in case of stomach troubles, he can only drink a small glass pure home-made wine.

The salicylic acid, which is used as a wine preservative, is not good, it's poisonous.

When you tell the intoxicated person that he should drink water, he replies: "Wine is made by God for us, and water is for frogs ". (…) Can you prove that the Lord has created wine? I know that water is from God, and wine is made by men. The Lord has created grapes, and wine is your product. Therefore you just recite, and you don't think. And they will take this wine, and make it "Christ's blood ". But the wine, which is to flow out of our tongues, is the reasonable word.

Ask any of the contemporary rich people how many times a day he must eat. He will tell you that he must eat at least three times a day: a grilled chicken, accompanied by a litre of wine, because the grilled chicken is no good without wine. "And then why the Lord has created wine?" This is a delusion! The Lord has not created wine. Grapes – yes, it is somewhat true, The Lord has created grapes, but not wine. The grilled chicken is also not grilled by the Lord.

There is a certain connection between water and wine. Wine is produced of the sweet water of grapes. It was said that Christ turned water into wine. This is not to be understood literally. There is a certain mysticism in the transformation of water into wine, and it is to be understood. The wine, which Christ made, was special. Such wine was worth drinking. Now you can't find a man, who can turn water into wine, like Christ did 2 000 years ago.

You've had communion before, but you don't know what kind of a symbol wine is. (…) Wine must get in and cool the life down. It has a great power, but because modern people are not prepared, it gets them excited – they don't have the necessary organisms to make use of it. When the wine enters the bottle and starts fermenting, the bottle breaks.

If man needed wine, nature would have provided it. Water cleans the body and wine brings in sediments, which one has to clean, in order for the divine energy to get into him. Thus energy enters through the brain, through the heart and through the body. As soon as this energy gets into man's body, it starts transforming him.

A religious person once went to the priest for a confession: "Father, I don't know what to do, I don't know how to influence myself. For quite some time something in me constantly urges me to drink wine. Whatever I do, something constantly repeats in me: "Wine, I want wine!" the priest was a reasonable person, he knew well the human psychology, and that is why he said: "If you want to drink wine, have some".

You would say that it is dangerous for a person to drink wine, because he may become a drunkard. There's nothing dangerous in that because from that very moment, a lot of counteracting forces will occur in that person. Various desires will appear in him and he will start thinking. Whoever thinks, he can't become a drunkard. If he drinks wine, a person can also drink water; drinking water, he can also drink wine.

You see some sins and errors in yourself, which are not yours. You want to conceal them before you. These sins are not yours, and that is why you don't need to conceal them. A young Bulgarian told me about his experiences. He told me how he became an abstainer. He told me: "My father was the reason for me to become an abstainer. He used to get drunk three times every week and beat up my mother." He was so shaken that decided never to drink any alcohol. So this is how he became an abstainer.

If it is about preference, it's better for him to eat a grilled chicken, than to drink a kilo of wine.

We are not against fire, but maintain the idea that fire must not produce smoke. "Is that possible?" If it is impossible now, it will be possible in the future. This means that we should get to the electric power. Only electricity can produce fire without smoke. For when you want to forbid someone's smoking, give him a superior idea. Tell him he can smoke, but first to fine a tobacco, which does not produce smoke and not to contain any narcotic substances in itself. When you say that, a new thought will arise in that man and he shall start thinking.

Drunkenness has its origin. The reason for drunkenness is in the human feelings — you block or suppress the feelings of a man, who wants to express himself. When a person has an ideal of sorts, or whatever urge and you suppress the expression of these feelings in him, then three urges occur in that man. The first urge is the occurrence of a desire in that man to tear down that obstacle – he will want to fight. The second urge will be the flow of strong grief. The third urge will be his desire to drink, to get drunk. Put that man in his natural condition and drunkenness will disappear. Therefore drunkenness is a phenomena, occurring as a result of suppression of human feelings.

If a young lad falls in love with a gal and they suppress their feelings, he will feel a strong urge to drink. Doctors treat drunkenness with various medicines, but the best remedy in this case is to replace this feeling or desire to drink with a stronger, higher feeling. The strong feelings of a man always replace the weaker feelings. Drunkenness is not of the strongest feelings.

The unachieved desires in the world, that, which cannot be achieved, this is bartenders pub. You will drink and pay. In this respect it is interesting that the one, teaching people to drink, he is sober himself. The bartender who teaches people to drink, he is sober himself. The bartender is the most sober of all, he can never be a drunkard inside his own pub, his is a model of sobriety! He says: "Hey Dragan, don't drink so much, a glass is enough!"

This man's name is Dragan, because Ivan can never drink. Ivan may become an eremite and cut a man's head, but he can never become a drunkard! And I will tell you why he can't become a drunkard. In order to form in someone, what is necessary to make him drink, you must first stop his motion. What makes one drink, you must put him in a barrel, it must not flow constantly, you must constrain him and it obtains the quality to make men drink. So Ivan has something, which flows constantly. Is there a fountain in the world, which makes people drunk. You can do anything, but you can never make wine from a fountain! And nobody has ever tried to make a wine fountain. You can make wine flow out of a cask, but never out of a fountain.

Why does a man now want to drink some brandy, absinth, cognac, vermouth? He says this: "… it's just a digestive". What will this bring upon him? All these drinks, which can be found in modern culture, will have very bad consequences in the future, in the birth of the new generations. There are people, who degenerate. The current world suffers from drinking too much wine. It will be very bad for the future generations. For people have to know how to drink wine. Here's what I say: we are discussing a matter, not in order to judge. We are only discussing the law.

If your lips are very thin, this shows that your sympathetic nervous system is poorly developed. Therefore there might be a shortage. Such people are choleric, nervous, they like getting angry, and they are usually dry. And if your lips are too thick, they you like to please yourselves, to eat and drink a lot. All those who like to drink, have thick lips. There are desires, originating from the sympathetic nervous system.

Here's what I say: a drunkard can be taught not to drink, but you must know how. An experiment can be made, but it takes a lot of time. You must touch his upper or lower lips in a certain manner, and he will gradually learn not to drink. You will wake in him the normal desire to drink water, and not brandy or wine. Or I would heal somebody, who wants to drink wine — I have never told this remedy yet, I will tell you now, but you should never tell anybody. So you have a person, who wants to drink wine, and want to heal him — while he is sleeping, take a sponge and water his lips with it. When you do that for a year, the original urge to drink water, and not wine, will be restored in him. When he started drinking wine, he forgot the taste of water. Therefore if you water his lips, the desire to drink more water will arise in him. You can try that on you sometime: if you want to drink wine, take a sponge, water your lips and you will see what effect will that have. Some sick people, when not feeling well, they water their lips.

How can drunkenness be healed? Make the drunkard drink 2—3 litres of water every day he will be healed. In the process of heeling healing, he must start from the smallest amount of water and gradually increase it: the first day he may only drink a glass of water, on the second day – two glasses, on the third day – 3 glasses, then 4, 5, 6 glasses, until he reaches 15-20 glasses every day. If he fulfils these instructions, soon he will stop using spirits. When a drunkard starts to like water, he will stop drinking wine and brandy.

Some ask, why people don't accept the truth. That is because their taste is distorted. Make a pub and sell water – nobody will come then, very few people will appear. They say: "This is destiny. That is how it has to be." When a person drinks wine, I don't judge him – I say: "This man is a comedy". He thinks that when he drinks wine, he will acquire something. I see that he is going to lose even that which he now has. Because in comedy the bar-keeper always wins, and customers always loose. In drama there is abstention. Where does suffering come from? When you decide to be an abstainer, for you have a habit, you look at the glass and try not to drink.

You abstain – this is the drama. When you finally completely give up drinking, it is the tragedy. When you give up all the bad life on Earth, it is the great tragedy, which will come upon you one day. When you forget about crimes, you will disappear from the Earth.

Trust in what God has put in you. Be joyful in the comedy of life, in the habits you have formed. Be joyful also in the drama, so that when you look at things, you laugh once again. How do you want to drink? I have given the example, about the person, who spent all his fortunes and then he became an abstainer. He read the Gospel and understood that he had to live a sober life. Drunkards won't inherit the Kingdom of God. He wanted to teach himself a lesson. So he went to the pub and said: "Give me a kilo of wine! Give me a glass of water! And fill another glass with wine!" So he took the glass of wine, put it up to his mouth, and then left it again down on the table. Something from within wants wine. E said: "Listen, for 30 years I listened to you and did whatever you ordered. Now you will listen to me – you won't drink any wine!" And then he took the glass of water and drank. The voice within said: "Wine!" So that man once again took the glass of wine to his lips and said: "I listened to you for 30 years, and now you will listen to me!" Then again he picked up the glass of water – drank it, paid for the wine, left it there and went out. And this is how he finished with that issue..

When a man drinks wine or brandy, he becomes a conductor of spirits, of irrational beings. Each thought, which confuses your minds, each desire, which confuses your hearts, each deed, which confuses your will, should be avoided by – you should not consume those. Don't accept a dark thought, or a dark desire or a dark deed either.

When a spirit talks to you, it does not talk to yourself, but to the others. It does not see you. It speaks to the spirits around you. Sometimes the spirits in you fight. Because many are sent from the other world. They send one, then a second, third fourth spirit etc., and they fight with each other to decide who is going to get in first. And you, not understanding the law, interfere with spirit's business. And whoever interferes with spirits' business has to pay. A spirit asks: "Why are you here? You are of the black." And another says: "You are of the white". When they say to each other: "You are of the white", you think that you are of the white. And when they say to each other: "You are of the black", you think that you are of the black. And you are neither white, nor black. The spirits are quarrelling between themselves.

So, many of you have entered this area. Some say: "There's something bad in me, which speaks". And I say: "When the spirits quarrel in you, just be silent. So that they don't know you. They fight, argue, and when they reconcile, when the black one comes, he will say: "Don't you have some wine? Wine from Malaga – French." A Bulgarian would come and say: "Don't you have 20-year wine?" or the spirit will tell you: "You must live, why are you so yellow. You don't live well. An soon you will pay, you will depart for the other world. Kill a chicken and make a soup with rice and lemon, and eating that you will gain some redness and people will see that you are well again." The other one, when he comes, will give you another diet. He is a vegetarian and will tell you: "Don't eat that. Teat good fruits, apples, pears, good cherries, then bananas, oranges." and then he will say: "And no butter. Just consume things, as they are. Don't cook tomatoes. Eat them as they are. Wash them a little and eat them. Don't eat that bread. Don't mill the wheat. Boil the what well and eat it." If you are a clerk, you don't have time. When will you boil that? In order to boil wheat properly, you need 4-5 hours. With the new, hermetically sealed pots, cooking under high pressure, the wheat can be ready in half an hour. Or you can cook at night.

You listen and you don't know what to do. These are desires of the spirits. If the spirits, living in the trees, come, they will say: "Listen, you will plant the seed into the ground." Others will come and say: "You should mill this wheat and sell it."

Yet others will come and teach you another thing; these others may say: "You won't live only on bread!" Can a man do without food? Of course he can. It is not the only way we now live.

Bad desires are always denser. A desire comes to you and clouds your mind. A desire comes, and the urge you have to work, suddenly disappears. Then you must know the laws, in order to free yourselves. The inspirations influence the world. Those, who have departed for the other world, your grandparents and ancestors, when they come, they can get you back, in order to convince you to live an old life. If you have a grandfather, who likes to drink wine, when he comes, he would say: "Why don't you drink some wine, treat yourself and treat me!" So you give him wine once, twice... then you become a drunkard. He does not drink, he is sober. He does not even know that he does not have a stomach. And when you drink, he is happy.

When a person is healthy, he may easily free himself, using his positive thought from the suggestions, of those who suggested to him that he was sick, and of those sinful souls, who departed for the other world, but –

being sinful –were not able to get far from the Earth, and continued to move between the earth and heaven, in the form of jelly, getting easily into people's bodies. Some mediums often get under their influence and act, as those sinful souls command them

Such souls are sometimes referred to as vampires.

The bad spirits, who have possessed you, may be driven out by fasting, prayer, force and knowledge.

If someone is possessed by bad spirits, the prayers and reverse passes are the salvation.

Spirits are afraid of hunger. Spirits don't like being hungry. Therefore, in order to free yourselves from them, if attacked – you must fast.

This is what the Bible says about the first man: "And the Lord made man in His image, after His likeness ". It was a magnificent picture, when the gods lived. The Kingdom of God was then on the Earth. Then something happened, a fall of those elevated beings. It is no known what the reasons for that were.

It is known, but I should not explain that to you. I can tell you why two man fight over one woman, and explain to you why two women fight over a man, but what good would that be for you? I can also explain to you why men drink wine, there are reasons for that. Nothings happens without a reason. A man always starts drinking wine out of lovelessness. Everyone who is disappointed in love, becomes a drunkard. Everyone, who accepts Love, becomes a sober person. Sobriety without Love is impossible. Now people preach abstention. Abstention must come to the reason. Love is to be put into the human soul and that man will then be sober. This applies also to vegetarianism. In order for one to be an abstainer, or to be a vegetarian, or a fruit-eater, he must have Love. It is Love that will bring the necessary nutritional materials, substances. Love is the best food. Eternal love depends on Love. The shortest love depends on hope. When you loose Love, you enter into faith. When you loose faith, you go down to hope. When you get down to hope – this is the lowest position. All the creatures, even the smallest ones, have started with hope, then ascended into faith and came to Love.

There is a law that you will experience before long. You haven't experienced that law yet. An angel will come with his sword, he will knock and say: "You are under arrest". You try to resist – and he sticks the knife into your chest. In the morning they will say: "He had a heart attack". The angel came from the invisible world, saying: "You shall come up there, you've been summoned". So he grabs you by the hair or the neck, or to say that scientifically: after he stabs the person, the soul comes out of that hole, so he takes out a bottle and when the person enters the bottle, the angel plugs the bottle and takes it to the other world. When he takes him to the other world, he says: "Seize him!" and, like predators do, they will form an union, they will form a body and say: "Why did you drink wine? What was the reasons for you to drink wine?" We, they say, have created water, the best thing, why did you drink of the other wine? Who permitted you to do that? There is a law that you can't live without water — whoever refuses water – dies. We imposed the "wet regime". Because in the spiritual world to drink water is the wet regime, and to drink wine is the dry regime. After you drink wine, your thirst arises, it does not satisfy your thirst at all.

The crime is in the fact that wine was not made by God. It is a human invention. Man took the Divine wine, and made it red. He lies and says: "I did that!" It is a lie. Let him make wine himself, and not take from the Divine wine and sell it as his own.

Everything, which obstructs the progress of the human mind is immoral. Everything, which obstructs human life is immoral. Everything, which obstructs human force is immoral. Everything, which obstructs human force – force in the good sense – is immoral. Everything that obstructs you from manifesting yourself as a person, is immoral. You must stay away from those things, which obstruct you. Things won't come to you, but sometimes you go to them. The cask does not go to the drunkard, but the drunkard goes to the cask. Does the bar-owner go to the drunkard, or does the drunkard go to the bar owner? Don't go to the pub, nothing more!

"We won't drink, we will obey God's law, we have will, will, will! We are living creatures, not slaves, and we will serve God!"

THE REFUSAL

It is not easy to teach people not to lie. The only thing, which nature now deals with, the hardest problem to solve is not murder, it is not fornication, but lie. Man will be free of all the other vices, when he is free of lie. All crimes originate in the lie. The lie is the basis of all sins. In order to kill a man, you must be very mercenary. When you kill a chicken, you say that you need its meet, and that if it does not die – you will die. You say: "It is better that it dies and I live ". This is also how cannibals think.

You have still not studied those specific deeds, existing in the current culture. A man's hair will turn white with horror immediately, if he sees how finely people eat each other now. These are the ultimate, bad results of the lie. We all suffer, for we subconsciously feel weight in the air, which presses us down. Sometimes we remain silent, we suffer and think that there is no reason for that. And this is the lie within, which tortures us. It is a horrible thing! The biggest poison, existing in the world is the lie.

How can you teach a wolf not to eat sheep? I have elaborated something: I will make an artificial sheep of chopped vegetarian meatballs, a ice sheep – and it will move mechanically. I will put some fur on it as well. The wolf would eat it in the old manner, but half an hour after that the wolf will throw up everything. After I give it to eat from that sheep three times, I will tell it: "Eat!" But it will reply: "I don't want it anymore!"

This is the law that is coming now. People must come to a repulsion. They must be repulsed by the old sins and errors, because they cause us thousands of sufferings.

When he eats meat, man receives from the animals such unnatural energies and elements, which take hundreds and thousands of years of clean life, to purge.

The reason for the sickness of people, is precisely the poisons of the meat food. In order to cleanse the human blood from those meat poisons in a natural manner, at least 10 generations of clean life are required. There aware methods for fast blood cleansing, but these are given to very few – only to those, who are ready to submit their lives to serving God.

The human food is fully dependant on his thoughts and feelings. Whatever his thoughts and feelings, this would be his food. Therefore you can't change your food, if you don't change your thoughts and feelings. Not only by their form, but also by their nature. If you don't change your thoughts and feelings, you won't be able to change your food either. If you can't change your food, you can't change your life.

All the meat-eating people, aspire to the centre of the earth.

Everyone who aspires to the sun, is a fruit-eater or vegetarian.

People of the darkness can eat whatever they want, but people of the light have no right to eat whatever thy want.

Many think that even if they eat meat, they can still be spiritual, moral. The wolf would also say: I shall eat sheep and still be good.

The beginning of the spiritual life is vegetarianism. It is also the beginning of education, because the spiritual life excludes violence. No one can be spiritual, if he is not vegetarian.

When it is said that man is to be educated, that his character is to be built, you cannot educate yourselves, or built your character without a musical thought. You can think of that literally, or figuratively. In both cases it is true. Each thought will cause an urge for some specific food. To like sweet food, sour food, apples, pears, eggs, beans, potatoes, all that is caused by certain thoughts and desires. Whatever the thoughts and desires, the same is the relevant food. Therefore, if a man has a broad, diverse thought, he will cause in himself the consumption of the finest food. The food will conform to his thought. His brain and body will be according to his food. This is what the future hygiene or the future diet will be based on. Good life must start with good thought. This is what food will depend on. For a person cannot eat a certain food, if he does not have a taste for it.

The Lord teaches people and spirits not to eat meat. When they stop eating meat, there will be no more death in the world.

The three of knowledge of good and evil is the meat food. Who must not eat meat? The wolf can eat meat – this I understand, but to feed the sheep with meat – this I don't understand. So, what is now better for you? To make errors and to sin – this is the easier food. And what is to live, according to the law of Love, this is vegetarianism. I believe every a person, who lives well is a vegetarian. And every person, who lives well, is a meat-eater.

If a person wants to have a pure and good life, he must abandon meat-eating for deep internal convictions, regarding the harmfulness of this food, and for moral conviction – not to take the life, which he cannot create himself.

Whoever is incapable of abandoning meat food, he cannot free himself from evil. Whoever failed to enter the causal world, he is not a true vegetarian. A complete vegetarian is only the one whose ancestors for four generations have been vegetarians.

A person not only is capable of giving up meat food, but he can also give up certain vices and bad habits. To give up certain feelings, which are very dense, certain sensations, which may harm his character, if you keep them while eating. And the mind must be fed with pure thoughts. And the heart must be fed with noble feelings. A man becomes what he eats.

What is the use of being a vegetarian, and not eat meat, if you have not changed your thoughts and feelings? Not only by their form, but also in their essence – if you have not changed your food, thoughts and feelings, you can't change your life either.

The true vegetarian must consume not only pure food, but also pure thoughts, feelings and deeds.

Everybody, who breaks the great laws of Love, Wisdom and Truth, is a meat-water. Everybody, who fails to fulfil God's law is a meat-eater.

In order for a person to be a fruit-eater or vegetarian, there must always be Love. It is this Love that will bring the nutrients, necessary for the body. Love is the best food. Eternal life depends on Love.

A man without Love cannot become a vegetarian. Without Love he is always a meat-eater.

The issue with meat-eating exists not only on the Earth, it is there in the spiritual world as well, where there are advance beings, angels, who has once fallen, and then – as meat-eaters, they suck out people's vital juices. Somebody is a vegetarian, but at the same time he gives money against interest. He does not poison his blood, as a meat-eater, but poisons his soul.

Somebody is a vegetarian in the physical world, but in the spiritual world he is a complete meat-eater — he is vainglorious, high-minded, suspecting everybody. Every food, which leaves many excesses in the body, and is hard to digest, whether it is physical or spiritual food, is inappropriate.

Which is the meat food? If you say an offensive word – this is the meat food. If your word is sweet, this is vegetarian, fruit food. Someone says: "I am vegetarian". Vegetarianism, fruit-eating is in all three worlds: in the spiritual world, in the Divine and the physical worlds. There is meat in the Divine world as well. Do you think that when you want to punish somebody, from the Divine perspective this is not meat food?

One must become a vegetarian in physical, mental and spiritual aspect. Somebody can be a vegetarian physically, but in his thoughts and manners, he may be not. In you feelings and thoughts, you must go in parallel with vegetarianism. If there is a single destructive thought or a single destructive desire – this is meat-eating. A new philosophy of vegetarianism is required.

If you, being vegetarians, want to eat meat food, you will meet death. The law is almost the same, when they want to turn a meat-eater into a vegetarian — he will undergo the same thing. It is not easy to become a vegetarian. There must be a transitive state in your food.

The danger of vegetarianism for some people, consists only of their having animal urges, while wanting to live like humans. A certain conflict occurs in the stomachs of such people, and they say: vegetarianism does not suit us. One has to be a vegetarian by conviction. Then he will be able to properly digest the food he consumes.

Some people have a good desire to become vegetarians, but they only have thoughts of no longer eating meat – nothing else.

It was during the summer, we passed through a garden, there were tables there with stakes, and he sighed. He thought: how good it used to be back in the days! And this is what is my philosophy: I tried to pass the garden as soon as possible, for it smelled bad to me, and he sighed.

When I speak of natural food, I don't have ay intention to impose upon you my understanding of food, but I strongly advise you to consume only food that you like, and that your body can handle. What good there is if somebody becomes a vegetarian and constantly peeks at the meat, feeling sorry that has given it up? It is better for him to remain a meat eater, than to be vegetarian and torture himself. When you change your eating habits and your entire lives, first try to see how the change will affect you. If it affects your body well, follow it. Otherwise you can return to the old way of life and eating. (…) A man has to live only the life, which can bring some improvement into his nervous system.

Pork can only be eaten as a remedy. Healthy people should not eat pork. The sick may also eat mutton, chicken and eggs. I consider vegetarians not those who sit in front of me and don't eat meat, but those who don't have a desire to eat, who don't feel it natural to eat meat. The meat food is very impure. Those who want to eat a lot of meat, especially when they smell it, it is because due to atavistic reasons, they still have the desire to eat meat.

A true vegetarian does not eat meat even in his dream. There is a world of astral mud – whoever passes that road – even if he is a saint – will get muddy. After that a man has to clean himself a lot of time, in order to wash away that mud.

Animals do not have good food. Only butterflies and bees eat quite properly. But they also lead unnatural lives. He is yet to begin learning. A society has to make that experiment. I have yet to find a society, which eats well and properly. I have studied the eating habits of the English, Americans, Germans, Russians and I see that they all eat in the same way. It is just now that there are some societies that want to use this new way of eating, but they do not now how to begin.

The people of the new— sixth race — will eat exclusively fruit food. Meat is a strong food, but harmful and it won't even be mentioned in the future. Meat-eating is one of the reasons for cruelty and rudeness of people, and for neurasthenia. Man will recreate his body through food. If he does not do that, he will live a long time with the animal urges.

The perfect food is fruits. The student must consume mostly them. They cleanse his body, thoughts and feelings.

Fruits are a rich literature in the invisible world and if vegetarianism shifts to a higher field, it will have the expected result.

Vegetarianism is the future method of eating for the entire mankind and that is why, who is now a vegetarian, he is in the avant-garde of the new culture, which is now coming.

The great spiritual warm wave, which is now coming to this world, destroys the ices and turns them into water. A thousand years from now, not only people will change, but the wolves will also stop eating sheep. They will be repulsed from the meat and will consume plant food.

If we eat wheat and fruit, our lives will be purer. When Christ's doctrine came to sprout in the human hearts, many people will go crazy and, just like old wine-bags, they will burst.

One day the wolves will disappear. All the meat-eating animals will disappear and they will be transformed. Spiders, eating flies, all the creatures who love meat food, will disappear, because that food is not healthy — that is it. It is not good for constructing the body.

Why are people allowed to eat sheep, and wolves are not? Why a wolf, after eating a sheep, may be killed by anybody? The law allows it to be killed, and when a man eats a sheep, he is not killed for that. There is a misunderstanding – the crime is the same.

So I ask: what is the future of the wolves? They have not future. And all the wolves will be terminated from the face of the Earth. And the wolves may not inherit the Earth. All the meat-eating animals won't heirs of the Earth – tigers, lions, cats, dogs – all these will be gone and won't be able to inherit the earth. And all people, acting in the same way, they will be gone too. The law is the same – they won't inherit the Earth either. However bad people will depart a bit later. Bad animals will depart first, and bad people will go away gradually, and they won't inherit the Earth.

Word

Doesn't food now serve for quarrels between animals? It does. The graminivorous fight over the grass, the carnivorous fight over meat, and birds fight over fruits. Where there are quarrels about food, life will be in an onerous state. Therefore, when we speak of the man, we understand a new situation of things.

While you are not hungry, the bread is free, then when you are hungry what will happen with the bread? So bread and hunger are alike. The bigger the hunger, the more intensive the attraction to the bread; the more hunger decreases, the further men goes from the bread. Can there be a low that when you are hungry, someone says: "You must not eat!" Hunger is a problem, which must be solved correctly.

The hunger exists now, because this problem remains unsolved for thousands of years. The problem about hunger has not been solved properly. For example, the problem about breathing has been solved more properly, than the problem about hunger, than the process of eating. You walk and think, but you don't think how to breathe, but think how to eat. You constantly think how to find bread. You walk about, but don't think how you can find air — you breathe constantly. Because man does not think about air, and does think about bread? What is air in this case? Bread is a condition, while air is environment. We are submerged in air.

One thing is true: all the poets, writers, scientists, who have created something great, were people of the Divine Love. They only consumed a little physical food, because they mastered a special law, according to which they took food through their pores, directly from the air.

Keep in mind that every organic food that you use, no matter how clean it is, always brings along its poisons and causes deposits. There is not a living person, who does not die, when it eats organic food. And humans started dying, after he started eating such food, because in every organic being there is clean and unclean polarization.

Eating, thought, work are not something material. Now there are people, who die because they eat in a physical manner. If they only took food spiritually, they would be living in the law of immortality. A person, drinking water spiritually never gets thirsty.

When somebody eats plant food, we say that this man is a vegetarian. You must know this: a person, eating grass, will start to resemble oxen. Whoever eats meat, will start to resemble the beasts, and whoever eats fruit, will be like the birds. Where is man then? So, if you eat grass– you are among oxen, if you eat meat – you are between beasts, and if you eat fruit –

you are among birds. This is a fact. What are going to tell me! Neither meat food, nor plant food, nor the fruit food have created man. The grasses will created the animal life of graminivorous, the meat food will great that energy in the man, which he uses to fight, to lead wars, and the fruit food will cerate in man the energies, which may be used for any feelings, for a thought. This is not yet proper eating. When he came to the Earth, Christ said: "Everybody who eats regular bread, will die and suffer". But whoever eats bread, coming from the Heaven, he will live forever. The bread coming from above is the human bread, this is the proper food for people.

The current philosophers have also come to this thought —the only eating man, is the one who thinks. A man who does not think, while eating, e is a graminivorous animal. And a man who eats and tears his food apart, he is a carnivorous animal. A man who eats and pecks at his food is a beast of feathers. If there is no grass, the graminivorous will disappear. If there is no meat, the carnivorous will die out. If there is no fruit food, the birds will disappear. And finally, if there is no thought in the world, the man will disappear as well. Therefore the only real thing is where thought appears.

Food is an object. This is work, which you have to do. Eating is a sacred process. (...) If you don't eat well, you can't understand the Divine order of things. The Word corresponds to eating food. When a person talks to you sweetly, you feel, as if you've had a good meal. After someone talks to you this way, you feel pleased. You say: "Forget about eating!" The conversation is so fine, that people postpone for an hour or two, the actual physical eating.

The more elevated thoughts pass through the human head, the finer food are they for a man. You live not only on bread, but with each Word, coming from God. A man's strength is in his thought. Thought feeds a man, just like bread. If thoughts are not healthy, no matter how much he eats physically, he will still wither. Whoever lives under the laws of Love, of faith, of hope, even if he only eats dry bread crumbs, he will still be healthy and joyful. God's Word is the living bread, condensed Divine energy. The wheat grain is one of the favourite children of the angels--, it is not something ordinary. The more you chew it, the more it gives.

The living bread is the understood Word.

Christ told his disciples: "Gather all the remaining morsels, for nothing must be lost ". With these words Christ wanted to put a great law in his disciple's minds. He wanted show them the Power of God, which is capable of multiplying the breads. Then He told them: "I am the bread of life, whoever comes to Me, he won't be hungry; and whoever has faith in Me, he shall never get thirsty". I think all the people, living during Christ's time, who ate from that bread, are happy for they still live now. You can find some of those 5 000 people, who ate from that bread, all around the world: in America, in England, in Germany, in Bulgaria — they are scattered everywhere. They can tell you themselves that they really ate from Christ's living bread. For 2 000 years they have been living on that bread. Can a person die, if he has eaten the bread coming from the God? Death entered life, because man stopped eating the God's bread. Eating is a process of the heart, and the assimilation, the use of bread, is a process of the human mind.

If you don't eat for 20 years, will become of you? A people, which is not in contact with God, looses its proper thought, looses its proper feelings, looses its proper deeds, looses its bravery, looses its foresight, looses its adjustment capabilities.

To acquired eternal life – this means to feed not only your body, but also your heart, your mind, your soul, your spirit. It is a method of eating, according to the deep teaching of Christ.

The potential human life differs by constantly taking something in itself. The kinetic Divine life flows into it constantly. The kinetic human life, on its part, constantly processes God's goods, flowing into it. This law refers also to eating: if the food that you take in yourself is not chewed well, spread throughout the body, assimilated by the mind, heart and soul and it is not turned into a dynamic force, to be used in the world for God's wok, then you will not produce fruit.

Sensibility increases man's capabilities of being healthier. And it is the mind, which continues life. If one thinks properly, he continues his life. The duration of the human life, depends on man's right thought. When you speak of happiness, do you really understand what happiness is? Happiness is determined by the right thought. Do you know what the right thought is? A thought is right if it is not afraid of suffering. The right thought is not afraid of hunger. For a man of thought, a month of hunger is just a good reflection. When the man of thought fasts for one month without eating, the thought can nourish him. He eats by breathing. He shall not seek food. An adherent of the first degree eats very seldom. He takes one lunch, one material lunch, during the year. During the remaining time he only eats quickly: like when you have work and eat quickly. He eats through the air, through breathing.

A book was recently published in English. A man tells about his experiences 20-30 years ago in India. An American went to an Hindu adherent, saying: "There's no bread!" "The bread will be here shortly." Then the adherent asked: "How many breads will you need?" "Five breads." so 5 hot breads came – so well baked, as if they had just come out of the oven. They needed radishes. Whatever they needed, it was found immediately. You may say that this is an illusion. It is not an illusion. It is said that Christ fed 5 000 people, using only 5 breads and several fishes.

Those of you, who studied the law of nutrition for a long time, use 50-100 grams of rice every day and they are healthy. You can live half a year on 100 grams of butter. And you can live an entire year on 100 grams of yellow cheese Christ was a master of this science — with 5 loafs he fed 5 thousand people and 12 baskets of crumbs remained. This bread came from the air, the bread multiplied, but Christ knew the laws, he was able, he had faith and love. He loved according to the laws of Love, Wisdom and Truth. Every person, who lives under these laws, will be able to do the same.

Somebody is hungry, he is anxious and worried. There is nothing to worry about! Let him get into his station, let him send his thought is space and he will see that soon after that he will received through the air a calming, bright, nutritional thought and his hunger will be satisfied. This thought is sent by a good, elevated person. A child comes back home and says to its mother: "Mummy, I am hungry!" Which one of you, as a child, has ever address God in his thoughts, saying that he is hungry?

When you are in a hard spot, say the following formula: "Jova e re". If you don't have bread and you find yourself in a hard spot, say that formula deep inside of you, with faith and trust in God, and the bread will come. But don't say that formula to anybody.

What food do we usually eat? You must first take food from the air. In the spiritual world there are no surpluses of food. There are no kitchens, pots or wash there.

If consciousness is alert, a person may avoid caring about food and drinks, as he does now, and when he wants that he will have it – every day, and it will be a specific, perfect food.

Here's what I ask: if God is your friend, would He let you go around hungry and naked?

The first thing you must protect yourselves against is the auto-suggestion that you know everything and need to know nothing more. You say: "I have learned and now I can pray". You know nothing yet! Have you tried, being broke, without a dime in your pocket, having starved for three days, to pray for bread? If at that point your bread comes, you have learned the act of prayer.

The life is not only eating, but also having faith. If you have faith in the Word of God, you may receive the necessary power and feel nourished. You are hungry and you have too little bread. Faith can increase that bread. If you have faith and know how to extract the energy from a wheat grain, you will be able to extract from a loaf of bread, all the energy that you will need for at least six months.

An adherent, who understands the laws, acts very reasonably, and with very little work, he manages to earn his living. If he needs an orange, he takes an orange seed, and within two or three ours that adherent plants the seed, a tree grows out of it and gives fruit. The fruit ripens, he takes the seed and puts it in his pocket. He can get the fruit he needs from each seed. He needs bread – he sows the grain right away, and makes himself a bread. These are things from the "Arabian nights", but they are real, experiments have been made to increase the growth rate of plants.

When a man eats his brad, thinking of the source, where it comes from, he connects to the category of solar beings, which send their energy to create the bread. The different beings send different energies from the sun to specific places. There are beings on the Sun, who are specifically interested in Bulgaria.

This energy, from which the wheat obtains its sweet juices, from which the apples, pears and other fruits, obtain their energy, exists in the world, and if you understand the law of comparison, you can go to the Vitosha Mountain, without carrying any food with you. All the food that you need will come to you. It will be enough for you to spread your cloth, and the food will come down like manna. If you are thirsty, just spread out your arms and focus your mind on God, you're your hands will be full of water.

Each fruit is connected to a divine thought. Knowing the thoughts, connected to fruit, a person may use the power of these fruits. It is enough to pronounce the name of the pear, for example, so that it comes to help right away.

Can the hungry, which has not eaten any bread for a long time, satisfy his hunger? Or the thirsty to satisfy his thirst? He can't. These are simple, external truths. Water is the symbol of something deeper in man, bread is a symbol of something deeper in man. That man may satisfy his hunger and thirst, but he will always feel that there is something else that he lacks. We are now dependant on bread. But the reason is our wrong understanding. One day, when we understand the Divine law of Love, not as an external force, but as power, acting within us, then we will be satisfied without having to find bread. The issue of bread works for itself. It has been settled, the same way as the issue of air. And you don't need to look for air. Wherever you go, you just have to open your mouth and won't have to search anymore. You don't need to look for light. Open your windows or just go outside and it will come. One day this, what we fight for - - food – will come alone, you'll just have to open your mouth and food will come.

A day will come, when people will only use their lungs and brain to eat.

In the future food will be taken through the entire body, through the pores, through each cell, without chewing.

The day will come when people won't eat any more lambs, piglets, etc. for these will no longer exist. There will be no more wolves either, and people will live in understanding, applying God's laws. This will happen, when water and food are already within man and there will no longer be necessary to obtain them from the outside. People will eat from within, the way the Lord eats. For now you must eat a little and be full of thankfulness – this is the most important thing.

Christ says: "The brad that comes from Heaven". This means from the place, where the life supply comes from. The true life comes from there. Some say that in the future there will be time, when people will live on light. Everything is in the light. If you can condense light, there will be food. Some scholars say that this is possible. It make take thousands of years, but this will happen. If, after a thousand years, people start living on light, this will be a success. But I think that 2 100 years from now, the necessary conditions can be met, so that man can live on light. When they tell you that the Son of Man will come, don't believe that. When people start living on light — then the Son of Man will come on the Earth – for it is said that the Son of Man lives on the bread, coming from Heaven.

No matter how prosperous one is, ultimately only dry bones will remain of him. When He says that people can live not only on food, but on any Word of God, Christ means the consequences of both types of food. He knows that whoever lives on the Word of God, he shall live forever.

Current people only want physical bread, fight and abuse each other over it, and they don't know that they can live not only on bread. Whoever lives on the Word of God, he can even turn stone into bread. Try and see the power of the Word. A quarter of a bread has so much energy that can be found in 7 breads, if one knows how to use energy.

Christ showed people, what true food is. One day the soul will only consume the Word. Whoever lives on the Word of God, will always be healthy. If he does not live on the Word, he will get sick. So, if you get sick, you will know that you don't live on the Word of God. When you consume the Word of God, you will acquire Love.

LOVE

Listen to the instructions of your spirit and the directions of your soul, so that you are always well! The greatest thing one can do is, when he has power, to give freedom to the others. The greatest thing a man can do is, when he has Love to give the people bread. There are two paths, on which all the living beings on earth walk: the path of bread and the path of water. The first one is called "hunger", and the second "thirst". The first one is called "the path of bread ".

Bread does never walk along another path, only on the path of hunger. Bread visits only the hungry, water visits only the thirsty. The same law is: life visits only the dead. Bread and water are the real side of life. When life wants to express itself, it appears in the form of bread and water. When life goes on a visit, it pits on the garments of Love, which is called bread and water. When the hungry sees the clothing of life – Love, he strips it down and puts it on himself, and when the thirsty sees life, the clothing of Love, he strips it down and puts it on himself. This is called thirst. Bread and water are manifestations of life.

You can't have any understanding, you can't have an elevated Love, until you understand the meaning of eating. If you don't understand Love in its lower expression — eating, you won't understand anything. Note that the most intelligent beings in the world know how to eat and how nourish themselves. The least cultural beings, which hardly progress, has eating placed at the lowest possible level, and they have no idea how to eat, they have no proper concept of nutrition. Only the advance creatures know how the eat.

And I ask: have you asked yourselves the question, why Christ took upon Himself all the sins of men? I look at this matter a bit differently, not like they understand it. There are many theories. Aren't diseases treated with food? Each disease can be treated with food, because people's sin came only through food; the man ate poisonous food, it brought in death. Thus Christ brought another food from the tree of life. Christ was the first fruit of the tree of life. He said: "Whoever eats Me, he shall have a life within himself". Therefore, when you ate from the tree of knowledge of good and evil, death came upon you. He then came and brought food from the tree of life. Which is the fruit of the knowledge of good and evil? The bad doctrine, evil brought death. The good doctrine of Love brought in life.

What hinders man in modern life is due to the fact that he is not acquainted with the magnetic power, working in the world. Thousands of names have been given to that power. The Gospel refers to it as "Love", „Wisdom" and „Truth". This is the power, through which God saves people. Scholars refer to it as "vital magnetism ", which exists as a strong connection between man's mind, heart and will; that connection exists among the family members, between communities, as well as between the entire mankind. Scholars refer to it with other names as well, but they say that for a man to be healthy, he must work in various manners on himself, in order to acquire that magnetic power. In order to acquire this power, one has to eat, but this is not enough yet. He must know how to eat, what to eat, he must know how to walk, how to move.

Eating is connected with the process of Love. Whoever is incapable of proper eating, he cannot love either.

The internal link, connecting the body cells in a regular unit, is food. Man has to eat based on this law. This law refers not only to the body of man, but also to his feelings and thoughts. When the link between body cells weakens, the body weakens as well. Love is the internal connection between the parts of life, so Love enhances and supports life.

Man's power is in Love. Everywhere I look I sea mutters of protest that the Lord made this bad, that bad. If you have Love, if you start loving the trees they will give more pears, more apples. Love the wheat and it will produce more as well. Love the cows and cows will produce more milk.

Everything you love will produce more. Love the sun and it will produce more light. The air, everything you love, will bring upon you its benediction.

You can't be pure without Love. If Love does not enter, you can't be healthy. If Love is not in breathing, you can't be healthy, you can't breathe. If Love is not in eating, you can't eat properly. If Love isn't there in each thought, you can't think correctly.

How would you know Love in your stomach? You will know it only through good food, which you always take. In order to have Love, you must take only the best, the purest food. If you don't accept the finest food, you won't be able to understand the Love of the physical world. Why do you have to breathe clean air? In order to understand Love in the spiritual world. Why do you have to have the purest thoughts? In order to understand the Love of the Divine world.

If there is Love in eating, then man takes in God. The process of eating is conscious and super-conscious.

People use food as much as they understand that God is in it. If, while eating, they don't include the thought, that God is in the food, that food is rotting and only brings them sickness and death.

God is hidden in the food, that we eat, but we still don't know that. There is a mighty power in bread. If you are sick, and think of a fine, freshly baked bread, of good things, you will soon get well. When you drink water, you will know that the Divine is in it, when you breathe air, you will know that the Divine life is in the air, when you take in light, you will know that God is in the light.

It must be known that the Divine world merges with the human world through eating. God has made the mouth and tongue so that this life can be taken in. When Christ said: "If you don't eat My flesh and don't drink My blood, you have no lived in yourselves ", He put a deep sense into that. The spiritual is concealed in the physical. The spiritual world becomes clear only through the physical, The soul is only accessible to us through the body.

Here's what I say: we must want to know God, who reveals himself to us every moment. A holy yearning for him must be awoken in us, as our Father and we should do everything for Him with joy and mirth. Whether we work for money or without money – this is not important: if we use Love, money doesn't make stains. For us it is important to perform everything with joy and mirth. Some say: "How much should I eat?" If you eat without Love, whether you eat a little or a lot, that food won't do you any good, it is not blessed. This is the law.

If someone drinks water and does not think that the Divine Spirit is in that fountain, he is a dishonest person. If he breathes air, if he eats bread and does not think that in the Divine Spirit is the air, in bread, this man is miserable.

Eating is the first communion with God, breathing is the second communion with God, and thinking is the third.

When we eat, we take the Divine Life in us, we get in contact with the Divine Power and the Divine Thought. Eating is the most sacred act in the world.

Eat with a great benevolence! Know that the life God has given to you, he has given you through food, and it passes straight from the God into you.

Several years ago a man came and said: "Tell me what is the best way for me to become good". And I replied: "Eat well. When you sit down, eat well, eat musically, so that you are pleased with what you do. Don't think of anything else, be thankful for the food, for having good bread. See the good that is in the bread, and make it transfer into you that goodness. When you eat pears, plums, see what is good in them. See what is good in apples. Sat to yourself: "The way apple is sweet, I will be sweet like it. The way bread is sweet, I will be sweet the same way." When you drink water, be good like water. What gets inside you, be like it, don't look for anything outside."

There is a law in the world: what you don't love, you can't use. You can only use things that you love.

And I ask myself: what makes contemporary people eat? Above all we still have not learned to eat out of Love. Because if a person eats without Love, this is violence. So something makes man eat.

Never eat food, which you don't love. The fruit that you love, acts like a medicine. The law is the same for looking, never look at an object, which you don't love. Always stop your look on what you love, this is healthy. Never listen to what you don't love. Two people start to quarrel, go and listen to them. Listen to a good conversation, listen to the fine conversation, and see it smell sweet. Whatever good there is, pay attention to it, if you want to be healthy. Never touch things, which are rough. Touch those objects, which are smooth, soft, which make a pleasant impression. They are harmonic and healthy.

Don't think that food provides power. If you love life, which is concealed in the food, all the cells will open up for it and accept it. If you don't love a certain food, you don't love the life that is in it, it will get in and out of your cells, without giving them any life, which is contained therein. This is to eat, without using the food that you take in.

If you don't love the food, it remains closed. If you love it, it will open up and give you something. Otherwise you will only take the scraps of the food. We eat a lot but use just a tiny part of the food. It is important what we use of it.

If you eat without Love, you only take in rough matter, and the fine matter, where life is hidden, cannot be used by you.

Eat with Love and thankfulness, in order to use the food prana. The prana is a vital power, which exists in every person, but in different quantities. Whose wounds heal quickly, he has a large amount of prana. No matter how big a wound is, if you put your hand on it and it is full of prana, the wound will immediately heal.

Eating is a process of internal harmony. One must love the food, he eats, in order to be able to use it. If you don't love the food, it turns into a poison for you.

If people understood what energy is concealed in food, they would make use of it. If they understood, by taking in food with Love, they would bring into their bodies the power, the life, which is concealed in it. Each apple, pear, plum, cherry, potato, conceal in them power, which may rejuvenate men. But everything is to be taken with Love, in order to produce the respective result. Love attracts life. Without Love life cannot manifest itself.

Love must enter eating as a method to transform energies in a superior form. If you eat with Love, gets inside you pure. Love will show you what food to use. At present the finest food is the fruit food, you should eat fruits until the Word starts being food for you.

The main, the basic law for eating is Love. To eat, only when you feel like it, to eat with Love and thankfulness.

Between man and the food, which he uses, there must be a certain relation — he must love the food, he eats, but the food also has to be disposed favourably towards him. This we call living food, living bread. Christ says: "I am the living bread". You will find this bread in all foods and fruits. If you look for the Divine, you will find it in the foods, and fruits. In order to connect with the Divine in the food, one has to eat everything with thankfulness and Love. This is where the philosophy of eating is. Who has managed to eat at least once in his life with Love and thankfulness, he has understood the meaning of eating. It is not a matter of eating diverse food, but one has to eat with Love and thank God for the great good, he is given. Then even the simplest food shall be blessed.

You can eat the fanciest food, but have you not Love, it is no use for you.

A housewife cannot cook a tasty meal, if she does not love. She must love somebody. Whether it is her beloved one or the kids, or the father - anybody. (...) She must love at least one of them and she will be able to cook the meal, to saw a dress, to be able to learn well and play well. If she has only one person to love, she becomes a virtuoso.

Believe only in those things, which have been given with Love. Only they have power. Everything, given without Love, has no power in itself. If there is no power, you can't believe it. This is a law, which everybody can try. Give a man a quarter or half a bread with Love, or two breads without Love and see which meal will satisfy him better.

When you go to a sick person, bring him something he loves.

The first thing in the new doctrine is that everybody must become a servant of Love in his thought and his heart, and in his body. So that when he goes to bed, to serve, when the sleeps – to serve, when he eats – to serve, to become a servant of God's Love. This is how the world will be corrected.

There is a great difficulty in applying Love. Do you know what it is? If someone eats too much, and another – too little – they cannot love each other. If two people eat too much, once again they cannot love each other. And if two people don't eat at all – again they cannot love each other. In order for two people to love each other, one has to give half of his food to his brother. This is how people can love each other. This is the law of nature. The mother, when she eats, uses a part of the food for herself, and gives the other half to her child. That bird - if it finds a seed – it swallows it alone, but if she is a mother, she would first give it to her children and then try to find another seed for herself.

What I have checked is true. You can do the test yourselves. If you have one whole loaf of bread, an ordinary one kilo loaf, when somebody comes and asks you for a part of it, give him half the loaf. After he is gone, my loaf is once again whole. The other man goes away with half the loaf, and if he gives to somebody half of his piece – his loaf will also become whole again. The one, having taking a quarter of a bread, if he cuts that quarter into eights, the loaf will once again be whole. The loaf is being halved and given away, but the loaf of the giving person remains whole. Good has this property: there can never be a separate part – good always remains whole. It is like a fountain, which never empties, whatever comes out of it, always comes abundant. I say: this is true in Love's law. If all the people served Love with complete faith, there would never be any insufficiency. If sometimes there is insufficiency, it is caused by lovelessness. This law is true. We suffer from lovelessness. All the diseases are the result of lovelessness, ignorance is in fact lovelessness.

Every time a person does something, there is always a reward. The deed itself brings a reward. Love itself has something that rewards you. You eat something – why? Food rewards you.

What brings joy, what brings happiness, what gives light, what gives warmth, what gives abundance and all the goods, all this is God, who manifests himself everyday. The bread that you eat – it is light, collected in one place. The fruit you eat, it is light, collected in another place. The water that you drink – this is light, collected in one place. The air that you breathe – this is light, and light itself brings life. It is in the light.

Here's what I say: kisses in the world are the carriers of God's blessing. The Divine is expressed through kisses. Who among you does not go to kiss the fountain,? Who among you does not kiss the apples? Who among you does not kiss the pears? Who among you does not kiss everything that pleases him? You may say: "I haven't kissed anybody ". This is the first lie. You kiss, oh how you kiss! Purified this way, the kiss already makes sense. A hug, a kiss – these are divine actions, which urge our soul to develop. If the sun did not want to kiss us, if the wind did not want to hug us, if the air did not want to get inside of us, what would our condition be? This food, which gets inside of us, sacrifices itself – it starts kissing and hugging us. Digestion is food's love. The scholars say: "The food is well digested ". Food hugs and kisses the stomach. That food, which gets inside, loves it. The food, which goes out, does not love it. Here's what I say: don't eat food that does not love you. If it does not kiss you, it will bite you.

In the world that you live in, you pay attention to everybody who loves you, who feel love towards you. You love a fruit, because it loves you, you have something to eat of it, and that is why you love it. The things that don't love you, have not prepared anything for you, and that is why you don't love them. You say: "I love pears", because pears love you. You love water, because water loves you. You love the Sun, because the Sun loves you. All the things that love you and you love them; the things that don't love you – you don't love them either.

Sometimes you think that by loving the apple, you give it something. It's the other way around – apples have something for you, they sacrifice themselves for you. They give you of their love. They enter our world. They have a desire, they love you. In order to get into your world, they sacrifice themselves, they die. These things enter the purgatory of your life, the customs office – the stomach. After that, whatever they have brought there, they take it to the lungs, to the brain, to the various centres. They start studying human life.

But I say: a rational concept is thus created. Now we think that the apple is not rational. These are just our beliefs. They are not rational, because we don't love them. Each thing that we love, is rational. All the things that we love are rational. Everything that we don't love is irrational for us.

A man builds his life on three Divine things: on the light of his mind, on the warmth of his heart and on the strength of his soul. Man cam upon the earth to manifest the good that he has in himself. If he is good, smart and strong, he will have friends. If he is not good, smart and strong, he will have no friends. A true exchange between souls occurs in friendship. If you eat a fruit that you love, a proper change takes place between you and the fruit. The Love towards a certain fruit is capable of improving its quality. If you eat a kind of fruit for several consecutive years with Love, you will see that the tree is improving. If a stupid person eats one and the same type of fruit for several years without Love, the condition of the tree will get worse. This is a law. The good and clever gardeners produce good fruits. The self-interested gardeners damage the trees in their orchards. Various animals, which eat the fruits, appear in the trees.

Based on the law of similarity, which states that similarities attract each other, everyone uses the life which becomes him, i.e. which attracts him. A man can attract to himself only the objects, which he loves. You can't grow flowers, if you don't love them. Flowers have a language of their own, which only those who love them can understand. The old Bulgarians knew that law and applied it. They worked their fields with Love, planted wheat and grew it with Love, and that is why they enjoyed fertility.

So you say: "These cherries are no good ". The reason for this cherry not to be sweet, is you. I have made tests – I planted watermelons, which were not sweet and they became sweet. I planted sweet watermelons, and they did not get sweet. This does not happen right away. The good gardeners, who have Love, improve the varieties.

Good feelings organize matter. For there are feelings and deeds of people, which play an important role in the sweetness of fruits. The better people become, the sweeter the fruits are; the worse the people – the bitter the fruits. These bitter fruits are due to the human thoughts, , feelings and deeds. The venomous snakes learned that art, when people were the worst. The cobra was created during times, when people lived very bad lives. Tigers have remained from times, when people lived very bad lives, they are remnants. Sheep are the remnants of times, when people lived very good lives and we – if we want to leave a future, if we live well, we will leave something: some good animals will remain, fruits will become sweeter, sheep will become better, wolves will become graminivorous.

If you can obtain food in the proper way, you have God's blessing. You can perform a test: if you have been waiting for 4-5 days for God to manifest himself to you, a friend of yours, who loves you, who hasn't seen you for 10 years, will come to visit. When you are in the greatest miseries and grief, you will start to bag, saying: "I will die hungry" I would prefer to die hungry, than to loose Love, and have food. Food without Love is nothing to me. Food, which does not give me thought, is no good for me. Food, which does not give me freedom is no good. Food, which brings you freedom is Godsend. We must free ourselves.

ABOUT THE AUTHOR

Peter Deunov, the Master, with the occult name Beinsa Douno (11 July 1864 - 27 December 1944) was a spiritual master and founder of a School of Esoteric Christianity called "School of the Universal White Brotherhood"

The various components in the Teaching of Master Beinsa Douno are set out and designed in about 7000 lectures of his, provided in the interval of 1900-1944. They were released in several series: lectures before the General Class, lectures before the Special Class, Sunday lectures, Annual Meeting lectures, Morning lectures etc.

He started with three followers, and these progressively grew to many thousand.

28005632R00060

Made in the USA
Middletown, DE
29 December 2015